CHURCH PROJECT.

 Biblical.Simp
Relevant

Stories of
Church Project

WE WANT TO CHANGE THE WAY PEOPLE
SEE CHRIST, CHRISTIANS & THE CHURCH.

CELEBRATING 15 YEARS
2010 - 2025

A CHURCH OF HOUSE CHURCHES™
A NETWORK OF CHURCHES

Published by:
Good City Publishing
602 Pruitt Rd
The Woodlands, TX 77380
info@goodcity.pub

*First edition printed by OnPress Book Printing

Printed in the United States

ISBN: 979-8-9894408-3-2

Book designed by Brian Hutson & Church Project Communications.

All stories within this book were shared by real men, women, and students of the Church Project family in written format or transcribed from previous sharing of stories through voice and video capture.

To the early, New Testament church –
Who met in homes with one another
Who were discipled and studied Scripture
Who cared for the widow and the orphan
Who gave generously with whatever they had
Who lived in love and devotion to the One
Who faced suffering with joy
Who faced persecution with hope
Who transferred stories through generations
Who gave us God's design for His church

WE WANT TO CHANGE THE WAY PEOPLE SEE CHRIST, CHRISTIANS, & THE CHURCH.

My husband was invited from someone who attended Church Project upon moving to The Woodlands. We were looking for a new church to call home. One Sunday after the New Year in 2016, I recalled taking one step into the church and felt the Holy Spirit. I knew right away this is where the Lord wanted us.
LISA KAMERER

CP means unconditional love to me. I have so much love and guidance in Church Project, from being discipled to discipling, from a broken marriage to the restoration of my entire family. I truly love Church Project.
DIANA DODSON

When my wife and I decided to make CP our home, the Holy Spirit revealed it would be a place for us to serve the body. In the early days, we were foyer greeters and got involved in Discipleship. That led to working the prayer table, becoming House Church Pastors, and later a House Church Pastor Coach. My wife occasionally prays during Sunday Gatherings, and I'm involved with CP Creatives. The Holy Spirit was right — we've had the privilege to serve in many ways, and I'm grateful CP trusts us to use our gifts to support and encourage the church. We are stronger because of it.
CRAIG DODDS, HOUSE CHURCH PASTOR

Church Project has shown me serving and being real with other believers can transform your heart to know God more clearly. CP has been, in a very real way through the hardest struggles of life, a spiritual journey that brings me a peace beyond this world could offer. I'm grateful for Jason and his family of pastors that have been an exemplifying example to all of us!
LISA GUTIERREZ

Church Project has truly been life changing for me and my family. The messages every week, bible studies, House Church communities, and serving opportunities have changed how I live. This church is filled with God-seeking Christians that inspire me and help me grow. I wouldn't be living my life and raising my children with the same passion for God without this beautiful church.
KYLIE GARBE

My family and I moved to The Woodlands just under 4 years ago. We had searched out Bible teaching churches close by and this was one that came up. We quickly got involved with a House Church and shortly after started hosting one. Our whole family serves in different ministries in the church, and we are happy to now call it home. The church is changing all of our lives in many ways each day, so giving back and following God closer is how we can say thanks.
ANDY THOMAS, HOUSE CHURCH HOST

"They devoted themselves
to the apostles' teaching
and to fellowship,
to the breaking of bread
and to prayer.
Everyone was filled with awe
at the many wonders and signs
performed by the apostles.
All the believers were together
and had everything in common.
They sold property and possessions
to give to anyone who had need.
Every day they continued to meet together
in the temple courts.
They broke bread in their homes
and ate together
with glad and sincere hearts,
praising God
and enjoying the favor of all the people.
And the Lord added to their number daily
those who were being saved."

ACTS 2:42-47 NIV

Contents

FOREWORD BY GEORGE BOOTH

Why stories matter

Stories matter.

They mattered to Jesus and they matter to people who follow Jesus. Church Project is a great story. It's a story that was being written long before the first gathering 15 years ago. It's a story that burned within Jason years before he gathered a few people together to meet under the working title of *Church Project*. It's a story that was penned in ancient times when God ordained our paths and orchestrated our place and time in His sovereign plan to build *His* church.

As we often say in CP, church isn't a building or programs – it's God's people, gathered in His name, to live out His purposes, in authentic and transformational community. The Church Project story is a cosmic collision of thousands of stories, told and untold, from across our city and around the world. We're a coming together of the beautiful and the broken, all pointing to Jesus and giving Him the glory in our individual and collective stories.

Our stories give encouragement and hope to the saints. They tell us that we're not alone and they point to the redemptive and healing power of Jesus. Our stories are still being written and they hold a mirror up to the ongoing, sanctifying work of the Holy Spirit in our lives.

And the story of Church Project is still very much in its early chapters. 15 years is a long time but we're also only just getting our permit, having been nurtured and steered towards this moment. As we look back in the rear-view mirror to see all that God has done in and through CP, we also look out of the windshield of faith to all that lies ahead. As we harness all that's been done and learned, we press on with confidence to all that God has for us down the road.

This book is a timely look back as we reach this key milestone in our journey, but as with stories recorded in Scripture, they should be used to give us strength for today and bright hope for tomorrow.

Were we to collate all the stories of Church Project from the past 15 years, we would never get to press. They're countless but they all count, whether in this book or etched in the hearts of those who have lived their story within the community of Church Project. And they all speak to the faithfulness of God as together, under the still working title of *Church Project*, we seek to change the way people see Christ, Christians, and the Church.

Enjoy this collection of stories in the Life of Church Project, and let's harness the hope they give us for all that is yet to be written by Him and for His glory.

GEORGE BOOTH, ELDER

Why Church Project matters

Church Project was an answer to many prayers. From the first time we heard this young guy teaching to a large group of college students at what was called Axis, we knew there was a man we wanted to be led by as a Pastor. Rob and I would skip out on the regular "old people" service to go to the college service being led by Jason Shepperd. Afterall, we were teaching in the college department. Students came from the church there and from other churches. The room was filled with students eagar to here the Word of God.

Later he left and began his ministry at another church. It was then, the pressure was on from us for him to start his own church. Thankfully, he listened to the Lord and not us. However, it was quite tortuous for us to wait in the interim.

We received a call from Jason to have dinner with him at Cheesecake Factory one night. Then he dropped the big news on us. He felt as though it was time, the Lord had prepared him to start a new church. Personally, I felt a sense of relief and overcome with joy. Finally. Thank you Jesus. Rob and I knew what a Bible-preaching man Jason was.

And so it begins. There was so much legwork – which Rob knows more of that than I do. But Church Project is like no other church I've ever been a part of. It's not perfect because it has people that attend, from our Lead Pastor to the Elders to the staff to all our people. But I've never been in a church that follows the New Testament model. Nor have I been in a church with so little conflict. Nor have I been in a church that is so generous, from our Lead Pastor to the Elders to the staff to all our people. We have such a giving church. Not just giving of time and service but love for each other. And not only within the church but for the world. We're a church that wants to reach others for Christ!

It was here with Church Project that I truly began to love others who had less than myself. It began on a mission trip to Haiti. I was heartbroken. I had been heartbroken in Guatemala before, but this time I spent longer in Haiti. My love for these people, which Church Project provided the opportunity to go, began years of traveling back to this country until the US shut down travel for US citizens. Yet, God has given Rob and I several friendships in Haiti that we still have today. Please take the opportunity to go on a mission trip if you haven't. It will change your life!

Biblically, we have learned more from expository teaching here than all our years of being in church. We have Church Project and Jason to thank for that. Not only have we learned more, but we have gained a desire to learn more on our own. Why wait until Sunday! I need more and I need it now. This thirst has been here all along but it is now as though I must drink from a cistern daily. Thank you Church Project for expository teaching!

It is here that I have learned the necessity of discipleship. In previous churches, we never had a set discipleship plan. This is a vital part of a believer's life. When I was coming out of a very difficult time, a precious lady stepped into my life and began discipling me. This was much needed although I didn't realize it at the time. Now, the Lord uses me in this area. I'm thankful for Church Project for seeing a need for this and continuing to grow discipleship for our people!

House Church is what we are. A Church of House Churches. House Church is a family. It's a good time. A sad time. A rejoicing time. A time to pray over someone. A time for discussion. A time to dig into the Word. A time to sit back and just let someone pour their heart out and cry with them. A time to break bread together. House Church is biblical. I love House Church!

Church Project has given me confidence to share Christ with others in my daily walk. Long before Good.God.Gospel. conversations came to be, the Lord spoke to me in a gathering saying: *What are you waiting for?* Not only has Christ given me salvation through repentance and belief in him, but he has *unbelievably forgiven* me. Through the learned Scriptures and the joy I have gained in my walk, I began to know I needed to share the gospel. There are people everywhere who are hurting, searching and need Jesus. I saw it modeled for me first hand by Jason on a trip with our families. His sharing of the gospel flowed out of his mouth so easily. I wanted that. Yes, I was jealous of that, but I don't think the Lord minded. I began to pray for confidence, boldness, doors to be opened and for me to recognize those open doors. God answered those prayers! As I shared the gospel it became easier. Had it not been from the example of Jason and the stories he tells on Sundays about his experiences, I probably would not be able to share the gospel now. And with Good.God.Gospel., it is so easy to pull out our phone if we need to. I'm thankful for Church Project for encouraging us to share the gospel with others, for that is what we have to leave for all eternity!

I've made my closest, godliest, Christian friends in Church Project. And I wouldn't trade them for anything. They are all different ages. They all love Jesus fiercely. They are a gift!

We've been a part of Church Project from the beginning. This is only the tip of the iceberg as to what this church means to me. I didn't become a Christian here, but I did fall madly in love with Jesus here!

GAIL RICHIE, ELDER'S WIFE & FOUNDER

INTRODUCTION BY JASON SHEPPERD

Just 40 people in 2 House Churches

Church Project started long before Church Project started. Sitting in my truck in an East Texas apartment parking lot, blocks away from my university, I prayed some words I remember clearly decades later. I was sensing God might be calling me to spend my life serving Him in the local church. But, inside of me was a growing frustration between what I loved about the church when I read the Scriptures and what I had known in the church up to that moment in my life. So, I prayed something along these lines: *God, if you want me to serve You by leading in the local church, please let me be a part of what You originally intended for it to be.*

That sent me on an unplanned journey to seek clarity on what Jesus wanted His church to be across all people, all places, and all times. I kept growing an insatiable curiosity about the beauty of the body of Christ.

Jesus said He would build His church, and I was drawn to discover His construction plans of the church everywhere I read in the Scriptures. Jesus said the church was His body, and my short science background caused me to look at the beautiful systems and structures He built into the body of Christ. Jesus called the church the Bride of Christ, so I searched to see how the intimate relationships of the people within His body were intended to interact.

This journey took me on years of hope, frustrations, dreams, and disappointments. I developed some clarity on what Jesus' plans for His church looked like in the pages of the Scriptures. After His plans for His church became more clear to me, I was dissatisfied with and unable to do anything else.

I kept repeating to myself, and to few who cared, and refining my convictions about the early church. I grew in clarity. I began articulating what I now call *eDNA* (short for *ecclesiological DNA*). Meaning, the DNA Jesus intended for His church in all places, for all people, and all time, to follow.

Once I gained this clarity, I left. I left everything that I ever wanted and had worked for up until that point. I left security for the future. I left all of my church and work in the church as history. And, I started something new.

Leaving was tough. And starting something new and unknown was even tougher. I remember it all like it was yesterday.

We had no money. We had no place. We had no people. We had no name. We had no runway to make plans. We had no security. No promises. We had nothing but some deep convictions and a little bit of clarity.

But somehow, very slowly, I started to share this eDNA, these convictions, and my plans to go after them, with a few individuals. They shared it with a few others. And over a few months, we cobbled together around 40 people who would make up the beginning of Church Project. I knew very few of these people beforehand. But these people were pioneers.

I like to tell people that, like church planters, very few people are pioneers. Very few people are willing to risk to start something new. Many people will sit back and watch and wait until something is secure. But some people are convicted enough, or desperate enough, or brave enough, or hungry enough... to step into the beginning of something with you. But pioneers or the rare people who can *remember what it was like.* They're the rare people who have rare stories.

Although we had early pioneers to help us begin, that same pioneer spirit has been a part of almost everyone who has come to Church Project. This place is a little bit different for everyone who comes here. Most people are stepping into something different than what they have ever experienced before in the church world. And since we're *still a project*, we're still forming, we're still growing, we're still becoming who we need to become, that same spirit is what keeps our church having that same sense of ruggedness.

We started Church Project on January 10, 2010 (1.10.10) with about 40 people committed to trust me and try this together. Then on February 10,

2010 (2.10.10), we started our first two House Churches. I spent that first month helping two guys get ready to become our first two House Church Pastors. I knew I wasn't a House Church Pastor – that wasn't my role. My job would be to pastor House Church Pastors. Their role would be to pastor our people. So we divided 40 people into two House Churches – one House Church on the west side of I-45 and one House Churches on the east side.

I went back-and-forth each week visiting between these two House Churches. Then, every week, I met individually with these two House Church Pastors. Beyond that, I was spending my time with a few guys who were volunteer staff members, treating our church like we were actually a real church, and having staff meetings like they were actually real staff meetings. These guys worked on Church Project a little bit, and they each had a couple of other jobs as well.

I also spent all day every day in back to back meetings over coffees and lunches, and many nights over dinners where Brooke would join me, having individual meetings with people who might have some interest in our church. I answered a lot of questions. I got to know a lot of people. Some people we met with joined us. Many did not.

I would also get ready for our simple Sunday Gatherings. We just started teaching through the gospel of Luke. We tried to form a little structure around what a Sunday would look like. We kept it super simple. And, we got to know a couple of local ministries in the city. That's really all we did. It's all we had the ability to do.

Through all of this, we have kept all of our values the same. We made sure that people came to our church because somebody personally invited them – not from something they received in the mail or saw on a commercial. This helped really protect our culture. Almost no one came to our church without first having had a long conversation and explanation about our church from someone they knew personally.

Out of desperation to grow or survive, we did not change our approach or values. We did not want to begin trying to attract people to anything other than what we had originally wanted to become. We kept teaching the Scriptures unashamedly. We kept growing in our generosity. We kept multiplying House Churches. We maintained our simplicity.

Somehow, by the end of the first year, 40 people turned into around

100 people on a Sunday. And, somehow two House Churches turned into four or five. Everything kept growing from there. Every year we seemed to double everything.

We started off in a little bitty warehouse right in the middle of The Woodlands by Market Street. 40 people turned into 800 people for two gatherings in that building. And we started sharing that building with ministries throughout the week that needed a space to meet.

After about four years in our first warehouse, we bought the old Kroger building at 295 Sawdust. The journey into the building was unbelievably hard. On the one hand, God opened some unbelievable and obvious doors and handed us a building that was previously unavailable. On the other hand, it was a fight of my life to get into it. But in that building, over about six years, our church continued to significantly grow. And our building was used for even more significant things in the city.

We outgrew that Kroger/Sawdust space and had dreams to do other things for our city that needed physical space, and the former Legends building came onto our radar. The Legends/602 building went from way, way, way outside of our price range, to somehow affordable. The stories of how that building was protected from other buyers (local and national) are epic. The down payment money was surprisingly raised. And we signed and closed on the building just a couple of weeks before COVID closed down the world.

Since then, in this physical space, thousands of pastors have come to our building from around the world. Many dozens of local ministries have used our building for their needs. Thousands of people in our community have had their needs meet through events and ministries in our building. And many thousands of people have heard the gospel, been taught the Scriptures, become believers, grown in their faith, and been grafted back into the Church.

We've had some years that were really fun. We've seen some incredible stories of lives changed. People have returned to following Jesus. People have come back to engagement in a local church. People have met Christ and been baptized. Marriages have been saved and strengthened. Families have begun being led to follow Jesus. Our church has been able to impact other ministries and other churches.

And, we've had some years that were really hard. We've been through some tough things that almost broke my will to be a pastor. There have been a few moments where I didn't think I would be able to come out on the other side and continue to lead this church, or want to do this anymore.

Part of my own spiritual formation has happened through seeing God build this church. My faith has been tested so much. I've been desperate so many times. I've been really encouraged, and I've been desperately low. I have had to find my hope in the Lord alone, over and over and over again. This experience of planting a church, and continuing to pastor that church, has been used by God to crush and form and re-form me. And the cycle seems to repeat itself.

I hear pretty often by people that they are encouraged by how much they've seen me grow. Growing personally, publicly, is a humbling thing. That means that people can see where you were weak before, and areas where you needed to grow. That also means that the people who have seen you grow have given you a lot of grace. They've been willing to let you grow along with them, while they're walking alongside of you. And likely, we've all grown a lot together.

There's a reason why difficult words in Scripture are used to describe this thing called following Christ together. Words like fight, race, soldier, run, farming, stand against... These are all pretty difficult things. All of those words feel really familiar when it comes to the story of the first 15 years of Church Project.

There are also really beautiful words in Scripture to describe what we're doing in the church. Words like body, family, beauty, hope, life, salvation, light, good deeds, good works, royal priesthood, holy nation, living stones, city on a hill, house, foundation... All of these words feel pretty familiar when it comes to describing Church Project.

This is a beautiful place. With incredible people. Doing phenomenal things. And *becoming something together* that Jesus intended for His church to be.

JASON SHEPPERD, LEAD PASTOR

ONE

House Church

We are a Church of House Churches. We're in pursuit of what God originally intended the church to be. It's not defined by a building or programming but by the way in which the body of Christ gathers together around Scripture, meets real needs and shares the gospel. In the New Testament, we see this model of church – a people and not a place – gathered in homes across a city, sharing life, and supporting each other.

This way of church, or ecclesiology, is still as relevant today as it was just under 2000 years ago, when the Church began.

This ecclesiological DNA we see in Scripture is comprised of three primary factors: *distributed pastoral leadership*, *decentralization of a primary place or pastor*, and *diverse, dscipleship communities* gathered geographically, not homogonously. And Church Project has pursued this from the start.

Two House Churches in 2010 have now multiplied into many dozens of House Churches across our city, sending out many of these to plant new Church Projects. Every House Church has gathered in homes weekly, shared life together, studied Scripture and met needs for one another. We have House Church Pastors, Wives and Hosts that are coached and cared for as we continue to grow and multiply more, healthy House Churches. This ensures that every person is known and pastored by someone and given a context where their spiritual gifts can be used to love God and love others.

These are stories from those who pastor, lead, and love their House Churches and how House Church has changed the way people see Christ,

Christians, and the Church.

———

I've been part of Church Project almost from the beginning and have had the privilege of serving as a House Church Pastor for nearly that entire time. Recently, I've had the opportunity to lead House Church here and help oversee its health and growth. During this time, I've witnessed people grow in faith, wrestle with Scripture, and become part of a multi-generational community where each member loves and supports one another through both joys and challenges. It truly is family.

I've seen men, through the encouragement of others, called to Pastor a House Church. Many lacked confidence, but it's been so encouraging to watch other men rally around them, build their confidence, and prepare them to lead. Once they step into that role, they flourish and realize the fulfillment of following God's call.

The same is true for host families who open their homes to serve the Kingdom. In these Gospel-centered communities, lives are transformed and directed back to the Lord. Both leaders and hosts are finding their calling, and it brings them great joy. Lord willing, new leaders will continue to step up, experiencing the fulfillment of living in service to the King and loving others in these diverse, discipleship communities.

ERIEK HULSEMAN, HOUSE CHURCH PASTOR

We started attending Church Project but didn't join a House Church right away. Eventually, we realized that community is central to who we are as a church. If we were going to be part of this, we needed to commit. Initially, we showed up once a month, but we recognized that wasn't enough. So we decided to go all in and began attending regularly.

That's when things started to change for us. We began to see the beauty in coming together as a House Church — seeing the good, the bad, and the ugly—and walking alongside each other through it all. When the need arose for another House Church Pastor, we prayed about it and decided to step up.

There have been so many transformative moments. Families in our House Church have faced lifelong challenges, but through discipleship and support, we've seen God do incredible things. I love hearing, *I met up with so-and-so this week*. That's exactly what we're trying to foster here.

Before COVID, my perception of community grew deeper. I was committed, but I didn't fully understand the need for community until we faced challenging times. It became clear that there was no alternative — this community was everything.

I want to be part of a growing group of believers, changing and growing in Christ, watching God transform lives. I'm so grateful to be a part of it, and I know He's in it.

PHILIP BUTLER, HOUSE CHURCH PASTOR

My name is Nancy. I'm Italian and was raised Catholic. My mom, a hospice nurse, didn't take care of herself and passed away after a surgery. I got very upset with God, asking why He would take someone like her instead of the *bad* people. I stopped going to church for a long time, but over time, I came to terms with her passing, realizing she had lived her purpose. I decided to start going back to church and eventually landed at Church Project. I love it here, and I'm never leaving. I even hope they plant more churches, so I have one nearby if I ever move.

After a few months, I kept hearing about House Church, so I decided to give it a try. I found Bill and Sandra Eaton, whom I knew, and from day one, they welcomed me like family. We celebrated birthdays, grieved losses, and served together. I serve with Hope Beyond Bridges each month, and last year, when I had two surgeries, my House Church was there for me.

When I was in the hospital, I felt the love of my House Church deeply. With 13 or 14 people praying over me, I knew I was truly cared for. It's not a fake love — it's real, and it's exactly what God intended. I feel like I'm living out His purpose for me.

NANCI TRINGALI, HOUSE CHURCH HOST

In January 2015, I moved to The Woodlands from Chicago, not knowing anyone. I went to Church Project the next Sunday, and within ten days, I was plugged into a House Church. I remember knocking on the door, and Kate Howorth answered. She had the same Chicago accent, which immediately made me feel at home. House Church Pastors do an amazing job of making people feel welcome and engaged.

Over the seven and a half years I was at the Howorth House Church, it became emotional thinking about how many people walked through those doors, whether they came once or 100 times. In 2020, Calvin Williams asked me to be a House Church Pastor. I initially said no — I loved the community I was part of and wasn't sure I was ready to lead. He asked again a few months later, and I said no again. But then, he asked a third time, and this time, I said yes. Looking back, I believe that was the Holy Spirit guiding me.

No one is perfect when they start leading a House Church, but God can use imperfection to tell powerful stories. Over time, I've learned that it's not about numbers. It's about the individual stories of transformation. One couple struggled with infertility for years, and now they're on the other side of it. Another couple is still in that journey, but being part of the House Church gives them support and a place to ask questions.

Looking back over eight years, I'm so grateful for what God has done in my life and in the lives of those in our House Church. Church Project has been a huge part of that transformation.

SEBASTIAN SPIVEY, HOUSE CHURCH PASTOR

Jenny Ann: We've lived in numerous states, and quickly learned that our church would become our local family. We've been hosting a House Church for almost a year, and it's thriving. It's been incredible to watch. I have an autoimmune disorder that causes extreme fatigue, leading to hospital stays. During this time, our House Church has blessed us tremendously with meals every night for two weeks and many prayers. Our youngest son, just four, has also been blessed. The support we've received has been overwhelming, and we've been blessed tenfold.

Jason: We don't usually ask for help, but so many have offered. What I love about Church Project is how real it is. It's challenging at times, but that's how it should be.

Jenny Ann: We come from different walks of life, yet unite for God's glory in our House Church. Growing up in a small country church, I learned how important it is to recognize and use each person's unique gifts. Jason and I quickly realized we have a gift for hospitality. It's not just about inviting people into our home, but making them want to be there. We hope we do that in our House Church — creating a space where people feel welcomed and valued.

Jason: It's all about taking that first step. Behind that door, someone will welcome you in, and you'll experience something truly meaningful.

Jenny Ann: Don't hesitate to get involved — it will be so fruitful for you, and you'll find yourself serving others and becoming part of a true family.

JASON & JENNY ANN BARBER, HOUSE CHURCH HOSTS

I grew up in church and embraced the gospel early on. But for years, I tried to be the Christian I was supposed to be, feeling miserable inside because I couldn't measure up. I pretended to be okay, but I was unhappy, depressed, and lonely. I searched for the community the Bible talks about but couldn't find it.

In college, I saw it as a fresh start and tried several churches, but I just felt invisible. Then I was invited to a church of House Churches, similar to Church Project, and after a Sunday service, I joined them for lunch. I remember telling my story, and everyone went quiet — they just wanted to hear what I had to say. That was the first time I felt truly heard and seen.

Leaving that community after college was hard. I couldn't find anything like it, and I gave up. I focused on working, saving, and planning my future, but life felt empty. I kept hearing about Church Project, and eventually I agreed to visit. From that first Sunday, I knew something was different. The people were real. They were crying, sharing their struggles — it was exactly where I wanted to be.

KIRSTEN RABALAIS, HOUSE CHURCH HOST

Living in Hughes Landing, The Woodlands, Texas, has been amazing. The community here really draws people in — both Christians and non-Christians seeking what God has to offer. People in apartments often move around, but this is a great time in their life to introduce them to Jesus.

In our apartments, we've watched people go from heartbreak to stability, finding new community and redefining their purpose through our House Church. It's incredible to see such change in a short time.

One time, a man thought he was having a heart attack at the pool and ended up in the hospital. We were able to support him and have God conversations with him. The best part is the follow-up — since we live in the same complex, we don't lose touch. You can continue those conversations and show love in person.

What's most fulfilling is watching people grow in our House Church. They go from being closed off, saying, *You don't understand what I'm going through*, to opening up and seeking support. It's amazing to see someone go from being spoon-fed to reading their Bible at Starbucks, discussing it with others in our House Church.

When we first started, most people didn't even own a Bible. Now, they bring their own, underlining verses and asking questions. The best part of Wednesday nights is when they ask, *Can you say that again?* or *How does this Old Testament verse connect with the New Testament?* Watching them grow hungry for the word and seeing the Holy Spirit move in their lives is incredible.

At the end of the day, it's all about loving one another.

JOSH KEOUGH, HOUSE CHURCH PASTOR

We started our House Church as an idea, recognizing a need for one closer to Houston. After discussing with leadership and going through training, we planted a House Church downtown. It's amazing to see people in Houston, some who've never heard of Church Project, find community in our House Church.

Our House Church goes beyond just Wednesday meetings. We share meals, attend each other's showers, and meet outside of regular gatherings. We bond over our shared love for Jesus, and it's beautiful to see people of all ages and life stages coming together. We're united by a passion to deepen our relationship with Jesus and learn more about His word.

The most rewarding part is seeing people grow. It's incredible to witness Jesus change lives within our House Church. We've also chosen to serve together, recently participating in Hope on the Bridges, where we served the homeless around Houston.

One thing I love is how welcoming our House Church is. From the moment you walk in, there's always someone smiling, ready to make you feel at home. That's the heart of building a true community.

House Churches need a Pastor who is committed, who knows each person's journey with Jesus and shepherds them. While going to church on Sundays is important, it's in House Church that spiritual growth and discipleship truly happen. This is evident in all House Churches.

COLE HERRING, HOUSE CHURCH PASTOR

Our experience with House Church began before we even moved to The Woodlands. In 2016, we had a major house fire, and a House Church community of friends rallied around us, even though they didn't know us. That was when we first saw the beauty of House Church and the power of community. We knew we wanted to be part of something like that.

When we moved here and got involved in a House Church, it became a place where we truly felt at home. For us, these were our people. We've seen God move powerfully in our House Church, with people from different faiths coming to know Jesus and experience real transformation. Watching entire families come to Christ has been incredible.

In our House Church, there are people who have experienced more than we have, and it's been amazing to learn from their wisdom. But we also get to walk alongside others on their journeys. It's not about common interests like football or shopping; it's about the commonality of Christ, the Gospel, and the word of God.

If you're unsure, just try it. You might already have a community, but you may also be the one to offer that community to others who need it. And along the way, you might just have some fun too.

JUSTIN & KELLEY RAMSEY, HOUSE CHURCH PASTOR & WIFE

I grew up in three different churches but wasn't very involved. At seven, my dad told me about Jesus, and something clicked. I asked him to pray with me to accept Jesus. But I didn't truly follow Him until after high school, when I met new friends who introduced me to House Church. Will, my House Church Pastor, became a key figure in my life. He was the first leader who taught me how to be a man. At 21, he took me under his wing, and I saw how he worked and treated his family. Getting to know him and others changed the way I lived, including the words I spoke.

I love reflecting on how we can never love God as much as He loves us. How would God respond to me? Usually, it's with gentle truth and a reminder of who He is. I think about Mary and Joseph letting Jesus go, knowing what He would endure. It's painful to watch my daughter fall, and God watched His Son suffer for people who mocked Him — including me. Without God changing me through His Son and the Holy Spirit, I wouldn't have my wife, Nora, or my family. The gift of Jesus points me back to Him and reminds me of His love.

ANDREW MENEES

Life was good growing up, but I never felt *good enough* despite doing everything right. My dad was in the army, and even after the divorce, life didn't change much until he moved home when I was in junior high. Suddenly, I had two homes. I was focused on pleasing people and doing well in school, but I wasn't a believer. I met someone who was going to church, and for some reason, I kept going with him. I asked my mom to go to the adult service while I went to the kids' program, and we got baptized together, along with my brother. It shifted from something I did to something that became a part of me.

When I went to college, I learned about serving and being part of the body of Christ. Coming home, I didn't feel the same, but a friend invited me to Church Project. At first, I resisted, but when she said, *This is the more you're looking for,* I decided to go. I've never looked back. I believe as believers, we're meant to be together, and I've gained so much from others' gifts. Hopefully, I give a little in return. My role in God's church is to seek out those who are missing, and to go find those who haven't yet heard. It's beautiful to see Him build His church, and I'm honored to be part of it.

JASMINE MITCHELL

My dad was my hero, my friend, and my coach. We spent countless hours together — racing go-karts, playing soccer, and just bonding. He taught me that love is about spending time together. When his business struggled, he asked me to pray for him. I prayed for his business, but more importantly, I prayed that he would find Jesus.

In January, I got a call from my sister saying my dad's health had taken a turn for the worse. I rushed to see him, but my flight was delayed. On the phone, I thanked him for being a great father, and he told me he was proud of me. When I arrived, I went to his side, kissed his forehead, and asked if he understood the truth of Jesus' sacrifice. He nodded in response, and I told him I was proud of him. I said, *I'll see you on the other side, Dad.* Around 9:00, my dad passed away.

It was the hardest moment of my life, but thankfully, I had the church. The body of believers surrounded me with prayer and encouragement. Our House Church was especially there for us. For three years, my wife and I had served others, and now we were on the receiving end of that love. The church gathered an offering for us, and though we didn't need it, they insisted. It was a beautiful reminder that we are all one phone call away from bad news, and it's vital to be planted on solid ground. Through this, I saw the body of Christ hold us up in a time of need.

JOSE DE LEON, HOUSE CHURCH PASTOR

My name is Toks, and I moved to Houston in 2002. We were looking for a church, and my wife mentioned a friend who radiated peace from Christ. That's how we found Church Project. We wanted to make connections, so we joined a House Church just before the pandemic. When it paused, we felt blessed by what was going on in our lives and decided to open our home and host a House Church if God gave us the opportunity. It was intimidating at first, but it became one of the best decisions we made.

A few months ago, we had a week of discipleship meetings in our House Church, which helped us grow deeper as disciples. During this time, I asked my House Church to pray for me to have a gospel conversation with my mom, who had been sick for a long time. In April, I finally had the conversation, reading Bible verses like John 3:16. To my surprise, she was very attentive and asked for a Bible to continue the conversation. The next morning, she asked for her Bible to read those verses. Hours later, she passed away. I felt so blessed to have had that conversation with her.

Afterward, my House Church gathered, prayed with me, and I shared my testimony. It was unbelievable to be surrounded by people who had strengthened me through prayer and support, allowing me to have that moment with my mom. We study, support, and grow together in House Church, sharing each other's pain and joy. I'm so thankful for the community that God has placed around me. It's beautiful.

TOKS OMONIWA, HOUSE CHURCH HOST

In my early 20s, even while battling lupus, I was living for the moment. My relationship with God was weak, and I wasn't doing anything to strengthen it. Lupus is an autoimmune disease that causes severe joint pain, organ damage, and kidney failure. I endured chemo, dialysis, and constant pain, but I kept pretending everything was fine when asked.

There is beauty in the struggle, though, and I now see how God led me back on the right path. Three years ago, I prayed, *Lord, please place me in the right situation with the right people.* That's when I met Joe and Carrie, who hosted House Church. They saw my daily struggle and helped me spread the word about needing a kidney donor.

Through House Church, I met Taylor, who felt called by God to test for me. Even though she wasn't a match, she didn't stop there — she joined a swap program where her donor matched with me. She messaged me, saying, *I'm agreeing to do this because Jesus has given me life, and I want to give what I have.* Her selflessness and faith blew me away.

Looking back, I see that God put me exactly where I needed to be, surrounded by the people who would help me. His timing and provision are truly amazing.

NICOLE WOODARD

I'm a House Church Pastor, which is a bit surprising since I grew up as an introvert, despite being around people a lot as the son of a Pastor. I've always been comfortable talking to people but also need quiet time to recharge. What drew me to pottery was the handmade aspect, especially the process of centering the clay. When it's no longer fighting you, you know it's ready to work with. That trust in the maker is foundational to my faith.

Pottery teaches me that nothing is ever too far gone. If I mess up, the potter can reshape it. Sometimes, we want God to fix us instantly, but just like clay, we need time to rest before God can work on us again. I love how House Church offers a space to ask hard questions about Scripture and dive into the things we struggle with. As a House Church Pastor, it's been fulfilling to create a space where people can be vulnerable and support each other, especially in a place where community can be hard to find.

A passage from Esther resonates with me: *Perhaps you were born for such a time as this.* The part people often miss is the verse before it, where it's made clear that God's plan isn't dependent on us—He'll bring salvation through someone else if needed. We are invited to be part of His will, but we can't just stay still. We must move forward with courage.

JOSH WARREN, HOUSE CHURCH PASTOR CP WINTER PARK

My husband and I have been at CP for 6-7 years. It took us a while to join a House Church, but once we did, we found our people. The importance of living in Godly community became clear during a difficult time last year.

At 34 weeks pregnant, I was feeling unwell, but I thought it was just pregnancy. One morning, I struggled to breathe and coughed up blood. At the ER, doctors found a 12 cm mass wrapped around my lung. My husband immediately texted our House Church friends, and we prayed. Within minutes, we felt God's peace as we knew our entire House Church was lifting us up.

I spent 21 days in the hospital, undergoing surgeries, chemo, and a C-section to deliver Lincoln. After birth, Lincoln developed a pneumothorax and was placed in the NICU. My husband stayed with us at the hospital, leaving our 3-year-old son, Sutton, at home. I had peace about Lincoln and me, but I worried about Sutton. But our House Church surrounded him with love — bringing meals, organizing playdates, and sending toys and activities.

When I returned home, I began 5 more rounds of inpatient chemo. Our House Church continued to support us with meals, gifts, and most importantly, prayer. It was the true example of being the hands and feet of Jesus, and through it all, we felt God's peace and provision.

As my second round of chemo started, Lincoln was home, and my husband needed to care for the boys. My best friend, Taylor Petefish, stayed overnight with me every night during chemo. She decorated my room, brought food, and supported me emotionally while caring for her own family. I would never have met Taylor if it weren't for House Church. The Petefishes have become our family, and together we are raising our children

in God's love. It's a blessing to have such Godly support and encouragement.
AMBER SHOOK

Church Project has been the home away from home. Where i've forged deep relationships that extend beyond Sunday gatherings and where God has shown me my calling as a House Church Pastor. I've seen God humble me through the teaching and grow me in adoration for the things he loves. Truly blessed to be in a place that challanges me to be more and more like Christ.
LUKE PATTON, HOUSE CHURCH PASTOR

I came into CP at a time when my wife and I were in ministry burn out from 10 years of domestic missionary work. CP ministered to us by restoring and refreshing our spirit and soul. The House Church model offered connectedness and community that we so desperately needed to return to ministry and fulfill our calling and mission.
DENNIS MARK, HOUSE CHURCH PASTOR

Church Project has meant so much to my family since we moved to the spring area. The biggest impact that the church has had on us is our House Church. Without the people in our House Church we would be so lost. They've picked us up when we were down, and truly sharpen us every day. We are also grateful for Jason and the way he preaches. We have been a part of church's where the Pastor makes it about them or they don't focus on scripture and at CP, there is no gray area, just truth which is in the scripture.
TORI HILL

I've been in law enforcement for 25 years and have been part of this community a long time. When it came to joining a House Church, I told myself I didn't want to listen to other people's messy lives. Then, on Super Bowl Sunday 2021, I met Dwight and his wife Catherine at church. Dwight invited me to their House Church, but I didn't go. A year later, I decided to visit and quickly felt like this was where I was supposed to be.

After attending for several months, Dwight asked if I would consider leading a weekend. I was hesitant, unsure about the title and responsibility. But after a few more times, Dwight asked again, and I said, *Let me pray about it.* Two weeks later, the messages at church were about being obedient when God calls, and one week, Dave Edwards preached about getting off the bench and getting in the game. That was a clear message from God to take the step.

I've just completed my first year as a House Church Pastor, and it's been amazing. I now see how God worked in my life and led me to this role. It's about people's stories, and I'm grateful God didn't give up on me and had a plan all along.

JOHN SCHMITT, HOUSE CHURCH PASTOR

When my family and I moved to the area just 5 years ago we were mainly seeking a church that offered community. After our very first Sunday gathering we immediately visited a House Church gathering later that evening. We were welcomed with open arms, but also with a loving embrace that truly only comes from biblical community. What we found was so much more than what we thought we were looking for in *community*. Church Project has helped us to see God for who He really is – just, sovereign, sanctifying, merciful and gracious. We now have a better view on where God is in good times but also in the seasons that are pressing, hard and lonely. Just a few years later, my wife and I are now leading a House Church. We truly desire to lead people in a way that shows them who God is, so they can weather the storms while maintaining hope and peace.

BLAKE HUE, HOUSE CHURCH PASTOR

Church Project has been a true blessing to our family, showing us God's love through the church. We moved to the area for a new job, with no family nearby, and joined the Spivey House Church. From the start, we were welcomed and supported as we adjusted to life with a toddler and newborn.

When our daughter was born, our House Church blessed us with meals. When our toddler was nonverbal at three, Tandy from Project Abilities helped us navigate special education services. Project Abilities also made it possible for us to attend church without worrying about our son's needs — he was cared for and loved by the church.

Our House Church truly became our family in a new city, praying for us and offering support in ways we never expected. When we didn't have a car, Sherri picked us up every Sunday and became a spiritual guide for our family. We even spent Thanksgiving with her and her family.

When we moved to another part of Houston after long-awaited prayers for a new job, our church family helped with everything — packing, moving, unloading, and praying for our new home. Church Project has shown us how vast God's love is and how it can unite an entire church to care for one another.

BRIDGET BRUNNEMANN

Church Project to me is a continuation of a story still unfolding. I first came to CP 14 years ago at a Halloween Youth Event, invited by a neighborhood friend who cared enough to include me. At the time, I had just lost my father to a heart attack. I had no direction and didn't care to find one. But that invitation changed everything.

Through God's will and the support of the Church Project community, I came to Christ the following year. Since then, my life has transformed — from growing up in youth ministry, to serving in the military, leading students, becoming a House Church Pastor, a husband, and a father. I never imagined my life would unfold this way, but I know there's still much sanctification ahead.

God has been faithful, shaping my story since the beginning of time. He's always been patient, generous, and the ultimate truth in my life. He is the author and perfecter of my faith — He is who He says He is. Above all, God is Love.

I'm grateful to have a place to share my family's story and my own. The same invitation my friend gave me is the one Christ extends to you—an invitation into life with Him now and for eternity. This is my story, still being written at Church Project.

MATT OGNISTY, HOUSE CHURCH PASTOR

God has used CP to challenge, refine, bless, and strengthen us over the 11 years we've called it home. The simple, straightforward preaching has challenged us to grow authentically in our faith and share the gospel in our everyday lives. Serving in House Church has deepened our relationships and allowed us to live out the gospel through life's highs and lows.

Living in community at CP has strengthened our marriage, improved our parenting, and helped us form friendships that feel like family. Our lives are fuller and richer because of people who point us to Jesus and love us well. We are grateful for Church Project's focus on simplicity and the gospel. We look forward to being part of what God will do through CP in the next 15 years.

DILLON GOOCH, HOUSE CHURCH PASTOR

Our journey with Church Project began in 2015 after we graduated college, got engaged, and moved to Houston for Jake's job. We left all our family behind and wanted to find a church quickly. Jake visited CP first and loved the sermon and worship, but what really drew us in was the concept of House Church. Having been in a long-distance relationship throughout college and our engagement, we craved a community that knew us as a couple, not just as "Jake" or "Taylor." We wanted to build our life and marriage around God.

Neither of us had a strong foundation in faith. I grew up in a church where scripture was often sprinkled into topical sermons, but I never truly understood God's character. Jake came to know Jesus outside of community, believing he could figure things out on his own. Coming to CP made us realize how much we needed a community to challenge us and grow our faith. For the first time, we read through scripture in a church service and were amazed by how much we learned about God in those early months.

We finally attended a House Church in Oak Ridge. At first, we were hesitant — it felt awkward and intimidating, but when we arrived, we were warmly welcomed like family. We were immediately served dinner and invited into deep conversations. That night, our view of church changed forever.

Through House Church, we met Calvin Taylor, who invited us to lead a youth group at Project Students. At first, we weren't interested — we didn't feel qualified. But after a few days of prayer and conversation with God, we both felt called to say *yes*. It was the first time we heard God calling us to step out in faith.

Despite considering leaving Houston when Jake's job was uncertain, we felt God's presence guiding us. We prayed together and came to the conclusion that God had a greater purpose for us in The Woodlands. We didn't just come here for Jake's job; we came for His will.

CP has been everything to us. Since our marriage, we've been part of this community — House Church, Project Students, Bible studies, and Project Kids. Through the highs and lows, we've experienced births, deaths, weddings, baptisms, and graduations—all within our CP family.

Our journey into parenthood also reflects God's faithfulness. I had deep fears around pregnancy due to a past trauma. I was open to adoption, but Jake wanted biological children. As we grew in our marriage, I realized I needed to confront my fear. Through CP's discipleship program, I was paired with Melissa DeLeon, who helped me break down those mental barriers. With her guidance, prayers, and support, we were able to embrace the beauty of starting a family. Without her help and the support of CP, our family might not look the way it does today.

CP has been the catalyst for our faith journey. We owe so much of who we are, our family, and our confidence in God to the foundation laid by this church. The commitment to teaching scripture straight through has changed our lives. When we see the mission to *change the way people see Christ, Christians, and the Church*, we know it's not just a slogan—it's our life's mission. It's what we live out every day because of CP.

JAKE & TAYLOR PETEFISH

Church Project has been a place of true community for our family. We moved from California to The Woodlands in 2021, knowing no one. As we prayed for God's guidance in our move, we felt His peace, leaving behind everything we knew. Upon arriving with our two youngest, we quickly wanted to find a church. After attending Kid Week and visiting CP, we knew it was where God wanted us.

We joined House Church that fall, through my table group leader at women's Bible study. I'll never forget our first night — everyone was so welcoming, and I was invited to a ladies' dinner the next night. Though I didn't know anyone, I decided to go, and those women and their families became our family.

Before moving to Texas, we prayed for God to use us, our home, and our gifts to serve others. Two years later, after several House Church multiplications, we now host one ourselves. We've seen God's faithfulness, not only for us but for our children as well. He has provided a community like no other, and we can't wait to see how He continues to provide for His glory.

DEBBIE THOMAS, HOUSE CHURCH HOST

I grew up going to Easter and Christmas Mass, but never fully committed to God or His word. Life was easy — I never wanted for anything. In high school, I was a three-sport varsity athlete, but after tearing my ACL, pain medication was prescribed for recovery. In college, I tore my second ACL, and shortly after, I lost my best friend. I blamed God and turned to self-medication, using the painkillers for emotional numbness.

My wife, who had started attending Church Project, invited me to join her. I wasn't a church person, but for her, I gave it a shot. From the moment I heard the music at CP, something shifted. I got chills and teary-eyed, though I couldn't explain why. It was as if God was speaking directly to me.

Attending House Church made all the difference. I found a safe space to be vulnerable, ask tough questions, and grow in community. I'm thankful for my wife, who led me to Jesus. Jesus is hope and salvation. If you'd asked me seven years ago if I'd have a wife, child, career, and a life of faith, I would have laughed. But now, I see God's miraculous work in my life. Only God can transform hearts like that.

TYLER CASE

Joe and I were struggling in our marriage, on the brink of divorce. A friend's car accident led us to CP. Joe went to the body shop to pay for repairs, and Rhonda, confused why we were paying for someone else's accident, told Joe we needed to try CP. He agreed, though we had little hope it would fix us.

That Sunday, we went to church, just to say we tried. Joe later said it felt like Jason's sermon was meant just for him. From that day on, we attended every Sunday. While our marriage didn't change overnight, over the next seven years, we grew stronger by understanding what God intended for our relationship. The kids got involved with Project Kids and grew in their faith too.

A month later, Joe found a Wednesday night House Church, and a few months later, I lost my job. Devastated, we went to service at CP that Sunday, then to another church. We knew that wasn't our place, so we went to another House Church. I was nervous and overwhelmed, but we were welcomed and loved.

When Jason Hofseth asked for prayer requests, Joe shared everything that was going on. I was embarrassed, but it was the best thing he could have done. They prayed over me and loved me, even though they didn't know me.

We attended two House Churches for two years because we loved everyone so much. When our Sunday night House Church needed a new host, Joe and I said *yes*. We opened our home, shared meals, and built lasting relationships. Hosting was a blessing for us and everyone who came. While not everyone can host, attending a House Church is a simple way to build a community of believers who love and follow Jesus.

JOE & CARRIE BRUNO

Sarah: House Church has been a blessing. We joined to find community, and immediately felt connected. We were scheduled for a double date that same week and knew we had to stay.

Wes: It's more than friendship. We're like brothers and sisters in Christ — vulnerable with each other, learning from one another, leaning on each other through good and bad.

Sarah: It's not just on Wednesday nights. We support each other during the week — dropping off meals after births, babysitting, and just being there for one another. The connection is real.

Wes: We love hosting and leading. Both roles are equally fulfilling. There's joy in preparing for the group to gather; the house truly thrives when it's full.

Sarah: Preparing the house and meal takes effort, but the joy comes when everyone arrives — it's when we feel most alive.

Wes: We faced loss when a member, Solo, passed away unexpectedly. It was incredibly hard, but our House Church helped us process it, showing care and support during a difficult time.

Sarah: We've learned so much from the mentors in our group, especially on marriage and life stages. The wisdom in our House Church has been invaluable.

Wes: I can't imagine anything replacing House Church. With a Church Project Pastor shepherding us, we have real support — someone who checks in, celebrates with us, and cares during tough times.

Sarah: Sunday mornings aren't enough to fill you up. House Church gives you a deeper, more personal connection. It's not just friendships — it's family. Not showing up means missing out, and others miss out on you too. It's truly the best part of the week.

WES & SARAH COSSICK, HOUSE CHURCH PASTOR & WIFE

While standing on the landing in a cold dilapidated building, a couple climbing the stairs noticed us. Friendly chatter. Then the door finally opened and the five of us hurried through. My friends explained in English that they had told the couple we were meeting for a birthday party. Loud joyful singing ensued. Then, whispers from overflowing hearts began spilling out passionate prayer. They meet like this in spite of eminent discovery, arrest, torture and worse. *This* is House Church. Then I discovered CP was a church of House Churches. THIS is where I belong!

MISSIONARY IN MIDDLE EAST

My father is faithful. When the enemy tried to steal my innocence through my earthly stepfather, God's voice led me to tell my mom, and I obeyed. It was terrifying — especially since I had just told my biological father I didn't want him in my life. But the strength to speak the truth that day at nine was beyond my own; God supplied it.

It took years for the full effects of my trauma to hit me. On the outside, I appeared to be the successful, *good Christian girl,* following all the rules. But inside, I was a hollow shell, weary of pretending. I controlled everything to cope with the chaos inside, but I locked away my emotions in a box that felt too crushing to ever touch. Still, my father is faithful.

At 20, God stripped away the facade I had built. I fell into depression, panic attacks, and an eating disorder. I cried out to God, *Why me? I follow the rules and love you.* He responded, *Be still and know that I am working all things for my good.* I resisted, thinking God was mistaken, and life grew darker. The enemy even told me to end it all. But my father is faithful.

God led me to Job 1:20-22, where Job worships even in the darkest moments, saying, *The Lord gave and the Lord has taken away; blessed be the name of the Lord.* That wrecked me. It wasn't about me; it was about what God wanted to do through me. I surrendered, determined to be faithful as He had been to me.

At 28, I continue to be obedient, and God has blessed me with a community of support. My House Church, strong prayer warriors, and a loving mom and husband hold me accountable and pray for me. I even co-lead a small group at CP with Project Students. God is faithful, and even as I still face hardships, He is working all things for His glory. Amen.

MELANIE HOLLEK

I accepted Christ 40 years ago but my knowledge of the gospel and my walk has deepened since I joined the fellowship at Church Project 7 years ago. In addition, I have gained Christian friends and deep relationships with House Church members. Everything about CP makes sense especially living simply as a church so we can share more of our treasure and talents. I love the preaching and teaching at CP and I can't imagine attending anywhere else.

JOHN SIZEMORE

Our journey at Church Project started long ago when we met with less than 80 brothers and sisters in a building smaller than our current foyer. The charge to spend less within its walls and give more to those in need was what first drew us to CP. Once here, we quickly fell in love with our *biblical, simple, relevant* church. We were excited to be a part of a church that we could see described in the Book of Acts and the epistles.

When we think of Church Project and what it has meant to our family over the nearly decade and a half, we are simply overcome with gratitude. We are grateful for Jason and all of the pastors and leaders who have sacrificed so much for Christ and His church. These wonderful men and women have poured themselves into us so intentionally and consistently. Our fellowship and followship of Christ Jesus have deepened and expanded as we have learned to submit more areas of our lives to the Lord. We are also thankful for the thousands of brothers and sisters that we have had the privilege to worship with, week in and week out, and those we have lived life intentionally with through House Church. House Church has brought us rich, lifelong friendships and helped us grow as spouses, parents, friends, mentors, and Christians. Finally, the words gratitude and thankfulness simply do not begin to describe the mercies and graces our loving Father in Heaven has bestowed on us by providing us with people who have become even closer than family to us. This church has challenged, sanctified, sometimes rebuked, embraced, and given us true joy by allowing us to serve alongside it as the hands and feet of Jesus. We love Church Project and feel humbled and grateful to have been called here by Him; first as fellow rebels, and now as leaders and staff.

It has been amazing to see what God has done with Church Project over the past 15 years. We pray protection of His Church as we continue to seek Jesus first, and run hard after Him for the next 15 or more! We love you, Church Project. Thank you for changing the way we see Christ, Christians, and the Church.

ARON & STEPHANIE HARRIS,
HOUSE CHURCH PASTOR & WIFE

TWO

Sunday Gatherings

Our Sunday Gatherings are simple. Each week, we gather by the thousands to sing songs of worship, speak Scripture aloud, share stories of God's faithfulness, be still and meditate on God's Word, and study Scripture, verse by verse, through sermons.

Our gathering space is simple. Plastic chairs, concrete floors, exposed drywall. This reminds us to be *radically generous*. Our worship is *reverent and relevant*, singing songs that exalt the attributes and character of God, promote high Christology, and give unhurried moments to respond to God. And we've always been keen on a good hymn or two. We value the priesthood of the believer as we see families every week, parents with their children, take communion and worship together.

Church Project started with the prioritized values of being biblical, simple, and relevant. Since 2010, this has been lived out through our church in many ways, including a commitment to biblical teaching, every week, studying books of the Bible, verse by verse, unapologetically. You can follow along with current teaching, leverage past sermons and access more resources for studying God's Word daily. Sermon archives are accessible through the Church Project app, our website and all other major streaming platforms.

And we share stories of God's faithfulness, celebrate how God has advanced the gospel through small acts of obedience, and profile local and global Ministry Partners that we're proud to partner in their good work. In all these things, we maintain a simple, yet significant liturgy every Sunday where anyone can enter into our foyer, be met with a warm welcome and join us in worshiping God unashamedly.

These are stories of how God has brought people to Church Project, given us a space to worship and study Scripture freely, and connected us to serve His church and share life in House Church.

Over ten years ago, I walked into a dark room in an old Kroger. Songs were sung, the Bible explored, and communion served. My husband said, *This is our new church home.* The Holy Spirit whispered, *This is where you will serve.* Honestly, I wasn't thrilled with that idea. I thought the church was supposed to serve me, not the other way around. After all, it's called a *church service!* Well, not at Church Project. Here, it's a *gathering*, and I've been corrected a few times — with a smile, of course!

We've served in hospitality, prayer, discipleship, Creatives, and now as House Church leaders. Through service, I've learned the beauty of a dynamic church body and the importance of a distributive church that enables us to respond to the Holy Spirit. As seasons change, so do the needs of our community, inside and outside the church. A new, bigger building allowed us to quickly adapt to Covid and better serve the vulnerable in Montgomery County.

It was harder when I had to set aside my personal sadness when someone left our House Church to start a new one. I still miss those Wednesday night gatherings, but Jesus said, *Go and make disciples.* Sometimes we go, and sometimes we support others to go. We've been blessed to support four CP families who answered the global call to *Go*, each met through different CP connections — House Church, discipleship, prayer meetings, and the Israel trip.

I Corinthians 12:27 says, *Now you are the body of Christ, and each one of you is a part of it.* Some are the feet that bring the good news, others the hands, eyes, and ears. A beauty of CP is how it creates spaces for people to step into their roles in the body. It's not just one pastor on a platform; it's every pastor in every House Church. It's not only a Sunday morning welcome, but many dozens of open homes on Wednesday and Sunday nights. It's CP hosting Night to Shine with over 350 volunteers and Back to School better with another 200+ volunteers. It's 35 CP artists creating an interactive art exhibit to help our city appreciate Praying Through The Lord's Prayer.

1 Corinthians 12:20 says, *There are many parts, but one body.* Thank you, CP, for trusting us to participate in the beautiful, dynamic, unified body of Christ.

RAE ANNE DODDS

I've experienced God's faithfulness in profound ways at Church Project. Over the past five years, CP has become a cornerstone of my spiritual journey. Serving on the video team for the last three years has been transformative. Through this ministry, I've developed technical skills and deeper connections with fellow believers, witnessing God's work in our lives.

Every Sunday, as I capture moments of worship and messages of hope, I see firsthand how God uses our talents to touch hearts and spread His word. The camaraderie within the team reflects God's design for community and service. This role has strengthened my faith, showing me that even small contributions play a vital part in God's plan.

Church Project has been a beacon of God's love and guidance in my life, and I'm incredibly grateful for how it has shaped my walk with Him.

TREVOR PARKER

Our family has served in many churches, but something was different about CP when we joined 10 years ago. Jason truly lit a fire in us every week. He challenged us to stop being comfortable and take the Word seriously. It was unlike anything we had experienced. We'd been to churches that preached the Word but never with clear actions to follow. Pastor Jason didn't give us step-by-step instructions; he simply told us to follow the Word as it was written. That was exactly what we needed.

After being challenged by the Bible, we began to see things differently. We got involved in serving, but the biggest change came when my husband became a House Church Pastor. We weren't just pastoring; we were hosting as well. God knew this was exactly what our home needed. Our whole family, parents and five kids, thrived in the excitement of preparing, praying, and fellowshipping together.

During this time, Jason Pierce took on a Global Missions Pastor role, and we soaked up all his wisdom, attending every global meeting. We sensed God calling us to something bigger, so we kept saying yes. Little did we know, CP, House Church, and Jason Pierce would come together beautifully, creating space for us in the Middle East. We are thankful to Jason Pierce and to Jason Shepperd for preaching the Word without compromise.

MISSIONARY FAMILY IN CENTRAL ASIA

Although I grew up attending church, I spent my first 65 years living outside of Jesus' way. I hit rock bottom when my 40-year marriage ended in divorce. My sister, who had attended Church Project a few times with her son, invited me to join them. The service was held in what had been a grocery store, but it was the most beautiful service I had ever attended. I had never been encouraged to read the Bible and didn't even own one, but here at CP, the Bible was being studied in the service. That was something I had never experienced.

I got my first Bible, began reading it every night, and attending CP services on Sundays. Still, my life felt overwhelming. I don't remember what Bible verse or sermon stood out, but when I felt at my lowest, I cried out to Jesus, repented, and felt the weight of my burdens lift. I felt safe and at peace. It was God's grace that led me to Church Project and to my redemption.

I joined a beautiful House Church where everyone cared for each other. Before CP, I never told anyone I loved my church. Now, with deep conviction, I proudly say I love Church Project and my House Church. I am honored to be part of a church that works so hard to spread God's word.

SANDRA FREY

In 2020, after COVID, I met my husband. We dated for 11 months, got engaged for six months, and then married. Everything moved fast, and within a few months, we were pregnant. But even with a new family, I didn't feel whole. I felt like I wasn't the mom I wanted to be, just going through the motions. My husband noticed, too. He'd tell me Bible stories at night, and during tough times, he'd pull out his Bible to read and find guidance.

One sleepless night with our newborn, my husband found a church and suggested we check it out. When we walked in, everyone was so friendly. I don't remember the sermon, but I remember feeling in awe. They spoke about House Church, and I was intrigued. I heard that struggles are part of life, and I realized I needed to feel the emptiness to lead me to God.

My husband baptized me, along with Dennis. Afterwards, his dad said he was happy to see his son leading his family on the right path, trusting God, not just himself. My life changed that day.

YVETTE SCOTT

Everything changed in fifth grade when life got tough. My grandmother, who I was close to, passed away, and my parents began a seven-year divorce. This deep cynicism set into my heart, and by high school, I was a passionate atheist, believing Christianity was absurd. I couldn't understand how people could be so happy with something they couldn't see or feel. I thought life was about achievements, success, and money.

After graduating, I co-founded a drone company at 18. Starting a business was hard at any age, but especially at mine. I put all my hopes into growing the company, selling it, and moving to Monaco to marry a model. As I worked long hours, I struggled with sin. My place of relaxation was the gym, where I met Dave. Over a year, we became good friends, and our casual conversations turned into deeper discussions about God's love. One day, Dave invited me to Church Project.

I'll never forget that day. I was about 35 minutes late and sat in the back corner. As the service started, I could feel my heart cracking. I began to weep because I knew I was home. I didn't have all the answers, but I knew I was in a place that could give them to me. A few months later, I sat down with Dave for coffee and asked, *What do I do now?* He said, *Start with the Book of John.* I began reading and, three and a half years later, just finished the New Testament.

The Parable of the Lost Lamb always humbles me. I can't imagine the joy in heaven when a lost soul is found. I felt that joy here on earth.

NICK MADINCEA

Hi, my name is Helen. I was born and raised in Russia in a traditional

Eastern Orthodox family, but we never read the Bible or went to church. I came to the U.S. because my dad was diagnosed with terminal cancer. I had my baby on May 4th, and six days later, my dad passed away. My husband and I were separated unexpectedly. He had to go to Russia to sort out papers and was gone for an indefinite period.

While in Russia, he ran into a childhood friend who invited him to church. This friend shared his testimony, and my husband saw a completely different side of him. He joined the church, heard the gospel, and was baptized in November 2012. In February 2013, a friend invited us to Church Project. I initially didn't want to go, but my husband encouraged me to check it out. He said, *I love you, but it's time for you to learn the truth for yourself.*

We started attending regularly. On my fourth visit, I picked up the Bible and began reading daily. That summer, I studied the Gospels, and it was there that I truly believed in Jesus. I told my husband, *I believe Jesus is who He says He is. I believe He's alive, and I need Him. I see my sin like never before, and I want what He offers.*

At 33, I was born again, and Jesus radically changed my life. His love for us compels me to share His truth with others. You have to love someone enough to tell them the truth.

HELEN WALLENBURGER

When I was growing up, my mother was very devout, and I always believed, but I had a hard time understanding God the Father. I felt like I had to earn His love. At 16, I was molested, and instead of seeking help, every adult who knew about it swept it under the rug. I internalized it and thought I had done something wrong. After having my daughter, I realized I would never allow something like that to happen to her without taking action. I decided I would be the person every adult in my life should have been for me.

I reported the incident to the police. The officer told me the DA wouldn't take my case due to lack of evidence, but they'd submit it anyway. I walked out feeling I had done something for myself. Two days later, the detective called. The DA had decided to pursue the case after another person came forward, reporting the same man for an incident 20 years earlier. I felt chills and knew that was God's timing. I had carried my diaries for 20 years, never knowing why I kept them, but I submitted them as evidence. That was enough to secure a warrant for his arrest, and he was sentenced to 10 years in prison. I knew God had worked in my life, and I decided to find a church.

One day, I was at the hospital and met a pastor from Church Project. He invited me to an 11am gathering, and I attended. Dave Edwards was preaching about the fatherhood of Joseph raising Jesus, and I knew I had found the right place. I started reading through the Gospels like it was the first time. One day, while driving, I had an overwhelming thought about how much I love my children, and it clicked — I realized that God loves us as a father, infinitely more.

That shift in perspective eliminated my fear of not being good enough. I understood that I am good enough because Jesus says so, and I believe in Him.

MARY KINSEY, HOUSE CHURCH HOST

My name is Kyron. I grew up moving a lot because my father was in the military. My parents focused on making sure we had a relationship with God. They were both youth leaders and always involved us in church events. However, moving so much, we never put down roots in one church. Church became a place I went on Sundays, sometimes sitting in a pew, sometimes a chair, just waiting for the time to pass.

When I was 10, my dad deployed, and we had just moved to a new house. I put a lot of pressure on myself to be perfect. It was just me, my mom, and my sisters, and with my dad gone, I didn't know anyone at school. Church became the only place I didn't have to pretend to be okay. There wasn't a specific moment I found God — He found me. He became the emotional anchor I needed, and I knew I was going to make it through.

In college, I wasn't moving forward in my relationship with God. I was holding onto what I knew. During orientation, I met a friend, and we kept running into each other. One day, he invited me to a brunch hosted by a Christian organization on campus. It was the first time I experienced people being close, caring, and worshiping together. It was the first time my heart was truly on fire for God.

I always joked about getting baptized when they had a big enough pool.

The week before baptism, I was still unsure. Then, Jason gave a sermon on baptism's importance, showing your dedication to God and to the body of believers. That's when I made the decision. My walk with God grew deeper, and I realized how much He loves me — more than I could ever put into words.

KYRON TAYLOR, CP STAFF

I used to sing in a band and spent a lot of my life in bars. It became a way of life: work hard, play hard. I had my work self and my weekend self, and they were two different people. One of them, a monster.

On January 8th last year, Jason preached about *starve your distractions and feed your focus.* He asked, *What is your distraction keeping you from God?* I knew immediately what mine was. My wife knew, my House Church Pastor knew, but not many others. There was one thing I was holding back. I'd done well with House Church and Church Project, but I wasn't letting go of this.

Jason asked us to share our distraction with the person next to us. I thought, *I'm fine with this. My wife knows.* But then Jason said, *Not to the person who came with you.* I looked to my right, and I saw a man. We made eye contact, and as I approached him, my mind screamed, *Don't say drinking, think of something else.* But as I got closer, I blurted out, *drinking.* He startled, put out his hand, and said, *Hi, I'm Shannon.* I said, *I'm Chris.* He asked, *Tell me about your drinking.*

I said, *I'm a binge drinker. If I drink one beer, I drink 24. If I drink whiskey, I drink a whole bottle. If I drink wine, I drink two or three bottles.* He asked, *Have you ever been to a meeting?* I said, *I'm not an alcoholic. I work every day, don't drink during the week.* He looked at me and said, *Yes, you are.*

I thought, *You don't know me.* But then he put his hand on his heart and said, *I'm 25 years sober.* I was breathless. I realized, *God put you here. He put you in this seat, and He lined all this up for me.* He said, *Absolutely, He did.* He wasn't going to let me leave without info about a meeting. We exchanged numbers, and the next day I went to an AA meeting.

At the meeting, they gave me a book and coin and asked if I wanted to speak. I said, *Absolutely, I want to speak.* I felt God leading me. I came home, put the book on my dresser, and the coin by my mirror. I fell to my knees and said, *God, I can't do this without You. I need You.*

God has walked with me since then. Church Project has changed my life. My House Church was so loving and welcoming, just like Church Project. I asked my wife, *Why didn't you ever talk to me about this?* She said, *I've prayed about it and waited on God to get you.* And God got me that night.

Last week, at First Wednesday, a year later, Shannon was sitting across from me. He smiled and said, *Chris, you don't have any bombs you want to drop on me tonight?* I said, *No, I don't brother. Because of you, my life is beautiful.*

CHRIS JOHNSON

Church Project has connected me to some of the most impactful people I've ever met. It's been here that God has accomplished the most growth in me. My wife and I have been in the same House Church since we started attending almost 8 years ago, and they're more family than we'd have ever imagined.

I've been humbled by the opportunity to be one of CP's primary photographers for a few years, and I've been privileged to grow as a photographer and capture some of the coolest moments I didn't even anticipate. I've taken so many group photos, candid shots in the foyer of hugs and handshakes, wide shots in the auditorium (and even one outside, thanks to a hurricane), and intimate close-ups that I hope nobody noticed at the time. I've learned the importance of capturing an event without disrupting it. I accidentally captured a photo of my House Church Pastor's son having a life-changing moment at Stations of the Cross. I've seen Jason with his wife enjoying experiences and immersing themselves with their family in church events and worshipping God. I've been significantly impacted by what I've seen and captured.

I've had the opportunity to play drums with the Project Students worship team, and I've learned the importance of humility on a platform. I've been privileged to photograph kids and students learning to worship freely and openly, fully submitted to God. I've had the opportunity to engage with House Church Pastors and their people in discipleship, encouraging Good. God.Gospel. conversations. I've had the honor of working with an incredible staff and being able to leave in pursuit of my photography career with honor and dignity, knowing others were behind me. I've been so thankful to be a part of the online broadcast and camera crew, being behind the scenes on a few of Wes' story video, helping with setups and teardowns, and getting a peek under the hood of some really cool creative projects. I've been honored to see photos I've taken fill a big screen in front of a lot of people or make it into a printed book, and I've been so humbled by God using the gifts he's given me to bring him glory by capturing moments in the life of his church.

I've been welcomed, encouraged, and supported. Church Project is a church — a gathering of people who love me and help me follow Jesus more closely. And Church Project is a project — reminding me that the work isn't finished yet, I still have a long way to go, and progress is always worth recognizing. Church Project isn't done yet, because God isn't done yet, and I can't wait to see where we go.

TRISTYN FLETCHER

I'm a mechanical engineer. My year was okay, but it wasn't easy. We struggled financially, and we couldn't afford much. One day, a customer asked, *Why are you in Venezuela?* I was doing a YouTube live at the time and replied, *We can't travel because we don't have money.* The next day, the customer called and said, *What if I buy you the airfare? Do you want to go to the USA?* I was surprised but said yes. It felt like a miracle.

A little later, I met someone in a bakery. I helped them pick out some snacks, and they gave me a business card for a short program. I didn't think much of it and put the card in my pocket. Then, I served a customer at a restaurant who was wearing a sweater with CP on it. I recognized it from the card and asked, *What is that?* He said, *It's Church Project. You should go. You'll really enjoy it.*

My family and I decided to visit. We were the last ones in line, but when we got to the front, a friend of mine — someone I hadn't seen in years— recognized me. He said, *It's great to see you here. We'll take care of you.* I was amazed. It felt like God had arranged everything.

The next day, we went to a Catholic church. It was our first communion, and I was nervous. I asked Jason, *Should I do this?* He said, *Of course. Welcome.* I wasn't sure if it was the right moment, but I decided to take communion. It was a powerful moment for our family, especially for our youngest son. It felt like we were finally part of a family again, something I hadn't felt since leaving my country. Church Project became that family for us.

RAFAEL SOCORRO

Twelve years ago, we walked into Church Project just three months after I had a massive stroke. I was certain my days of doing ministry were over. I couldn't hold a conversation without rehearsing it.

We immediately fell in love with CP and started in a House Church because we knew we needed community. We had just moved to The Woodlands from Chicago, not knowing anyone. A couple of months later, Jason preached about how God used Moses even though he stuttered, and it made me realize God wasn't done with me either.

I felt led to work with ProjectKidsJr. because of the one-parent, once-a-month opportunity. I thought little kids didn't need someone who could talk — they just needed someone there. As time passed, I got better, so I moved up to being a Student Group Leader and eventually led a women's Bible study small group.

Church Project has given me a place to use my gifts and talents, helped me grow as a parent and disciple, and has been an instrumental part of our family. It's given my kids a place to belong, believe, and become. We love Church Project!

SERINA TRUHLAR, CP STAFF

A simple idea — be the Church — has grown into something extraordinary. Not a building, but a body. Not a program, but a purpose. In 2020, when the world stopped, Church Project didn't. I saw a team of remarkable people step up, rally together, and ensure that hope wasn't quarantined. The gospel reached homes, hearts, and lives in ways we never imagined. Serving here is a privilege. Watching God work through ordinary people to do extraordinary things is humbling. Fifteen years of faithfulness. And we're just getting started. Thank you, Jesus. Thank you, Church Project.

JOSH THORNTON

Growing up, my mom worked at the church, and I loved it. In college, we attended a traditional church, but I was diagnosed with Tourette's. It was hard to hear. I started having motor and vocal tics — 40 to 50 a day — and I was embarrassed, wanting to hide. I didn't know what was happening and was afraid of being judged.

I visited another church, and while I liked it, I wasn't fully invested because I was scared of people. I decided I needed a change. My friend Brenda suggested I try Church Project, and I agreed. I didn't want to like it, but I did. I loved the worship because music is a big part of who I am, and Jason's sermon was great. I decided to try the young adult group.

At large churches, people sometimes greet you out of obligation, but at Church Project, they genuinely wanted to hear from me. It felt amazing, and it helped me see Jesus in those people — how He wants to know and love us for who we are. It reminded me that the church body is here for us, to be fully seen and known, by both the people and by Jesus.

CHRISTINE GUSTAFSON

Fifteen years ago, in January 2010, our family began a life-changing journey with Church Project. After months of searching for a church home and visiting many, we struggled to find one where we truly felt God was leading us. Then, a colleague mentioned that their former youth Pastor had started a church, and we decided to attend. It was CP's third week, and from the moment we walked in, we knew it was different. The message was authentic and gospel-centered, the worship united our family, and the church's newness gave us a sense of belonging. We felt welcomed, needed, and confident this was where God wanted us.

Quickly, Church Project became more than a place of worship — it became our community. Leading House Church for nine years allowed us to build deep relationships and stay connected as CP grew. Through House Church, we experienced the beauty of sharing life and faith, which kept us rooted within this growing body of believers.

Our three daughters have grown up at CP, shaped by its teaching and the community's example of walking with Christ. The consistency of leadership, the depth of teaching, and the heart of this church have been a blessing to our family. Now, 15 years later, we look back with gratitude for how God has used CP in our lives. We're excited to continue participating in what Christ has in store for Church Project in the future.

JASON HOFSETH

Before coming to CP, I felt empty and introverted. My family and I were attending a mega church in the Spring area, but despite its size, I felt isolated. Though they had life groups, there was no real connection, and eventually, we stopped attending. I knew God should be central to the church, but I couldn't find Him outside my home. I would read my Bible and pray but longed for community; we needed a church home.

In 2021, my oldest daughter set out to find a church. She had a list, with CP at the top. After Jason returned from sabbatical, fired up, she came home saying she had found our church home. The rest of the family visited and never looked back.

In the three years since, we've grown in many ways. My daughter and I have enjoyed House Church, and while my husband was hesitant, he's now attending. The gatherings have provided the spiritual and biblical nourishment we all desperately needed. Jason is a Pastor, not a motivational speaker, and his biblically sound sermons, along with those of other CP Pastors, have been a true blessing.

I love having Good.God.Gospel. conversations with co-workers and learning practical ways to engage in them at CP. God is truly the foundation of all things, and CP has empowered us to have these conversations and follow God wholeheartedly.

AMESHA SHERMAN

In 2019, I intentionally turned my back on God after suffering several significant losses. I questioned if God was good. In 2023, I had an encounter with the Holy Spirit. I was in a dating relationship at the time when I clearly heard the Holy Spirit telling me to end it. I said, *No, I love him*, but He replied, *You do not yet understand what true love is.* The Holy Spirit showed me that only He could reveal unconditional love.

God used wise counsel and the Church Project community to reveal the abusive nature of my past relationship. I came to Church Project broken, having experimented with substances, relationships, and philosophies. But Jesus is the only way. I remember Jason praying that no voice or philosophy could save — only Jesus. Before Him, my life was meaningless; I was experiencing spiritual death. Jesus gave my life purpose, brought light to my eyes, and life to my bones.

I'm now part of a House Church and being discipled. Jesus has transformed my life in ways I cannot fully describe. I now have a desire to be used by God in any way He needs me. I'm looking into joining CP's global ministries and becoming part of the global declaration that Christ is Lord.

ASHLEY LAND

It's truly a joy to serve. I look forward to it more than just attending on the weekend. Over the 12 years I've been part of CP, I've served in various roles, but I'll focus on my time in the sound booth. My main role is putting the worship song lyrics on the screens. Before CP, when I was a high school student, I watched our main tech lead for student ministry to learn everything I know today.

A couple of years into leading small groups here, I saw our student Pastor frantically trying to edit slides one Monday night. I believed his time would be better spent Pastoring students or prepping for his sermon. I was also able to fix what he needed more efficiently. This was for the benefit of the students' gathering time. I continued to serve as the lyrics guy in students until the person over it in the Sunday adult gathering had to leave for a job change. When he left, I took over and have continued to serve regularly in this way.

I love serving in this role because I'm surrounded by worship music. As a follower of Christ, each song I get to sing feels like a pouring out of my heart, expressing my desire to draw near to Jesus.

EVAN LIS

I came to Church Project in June 2022 and was immediately captivated by the solid Biblical teaching and loving, diverse community. Church Project reaches out to the individual with great care and attention. I felt I belonged from the moment I walked in, and it was equally impactful to see others join in the same seamless way! Everyone is invited to serve Jesus, our King and LORD. All are welcome, vital, and included.

At Church Project, both locally and on mission trips, I've experienced the most beautiful and powerful expression of the body of Christ operating with love and joy as one, as described in Ephesians 4 and 1 Corinthians 12. This has deepened my faith, brought me closer to the LORD, and surrounded me with love and purpose. To God be the glory!

INGRID BENDER

I started hanging out with the wrong crowd in high school, using drugs heavily. After graduating, I went to college, my first time away from home, but my grades dropped, and my parents refused to pay for more tuition. The people I was around weren't encouraging me to improve. One day, I woke up to find out I had broken into a house. I was in a bad place, feeling empty. My stepdad suggested joining the military, so I enlisted in the Navy and left three weeks later.

During my time in the Navy, I faced many trials, including leaving an abusive relationship, being assaulted by my direct supervisor, and the father of my two children abandoning me. I returned home broken — abused, assaulted, and abandoned.

I had been baptized at 11 after attending a church camp, but I didn't truly understand or follow Jesus. He was just someone I blamed when I was angry or confused. My mom went to church sometimes, but my stepdad didn't believe. So I tried to form a relationship with Jesus on my own, without guidance.

When I visited my grandparents in Hemphill, they recommended Church Project to me. They said it was a great environment, so I decided to check it out. Two weeks later, I came to Church Project and my journey with God truly began. I will never forget how someone I didn't know immediately shook my hand and asked, *How long have you been coming? Do you have a House Church?* From that moment, they pointed me in the right direction, encouraging me to walk with God every chance I got.

Jesus knows what you need. He talks about having a community. He introduced me to the right people. Had I continued down the wrong path, honestly don't know where I would be without them.

CLAIRE LOGAN

It's hard to put into words what Church Project means to me because of all the feelings, memories, and life we've shared here. We came to CP in 2013 with our young family and were immediately welcomed by Calvin and Lindsay Taylor. That day, our girls began their journey through the children's program. From that first day, we felt a sense of belonging. Church Project answered so many prayers for God to plant us into a community that would strengthen our family and help raise our children with a solid Biblical foundation.

I remember walking into that first service, and the worship felt so raw and real. The intentionality of the service — moments of stillness, silence, and meditation — spoke directly to my soul. I wrote in my notes that day, *This is it. Our home church.* Since then, each year has been a new chapter of growth. As we uncovered more about CP, I realized it aligned perfectly with who we were and who God was calling us to be. The teachings challenged us to do more, give more, and dig deeper into our faith, often refining us in uncomfortable ways.

Through it all, the community at Church Project surrounded us, lifted us up, and kept us pursuing Christ. In that refining process, I found my identity in Christ — not in what I did, or what others thought, but in Him alone. CP provided opportunities to serve in youth, children's ministry, community projects, and worship, helping us grow into the people God intended us to be.

When our boys were born, our House Church family supported us in every way, from meals to prayers. They helped us navigate the early years of parenting, and I'll never forget how the nursery was ready for them when they were just two weeks old. Our children have been loved and cared for, growing in their faith, confidence, and callings. They've been baptized, gone on mission trips, and built lifelong friendships, all here at CP.

I'm deeply grateful for the leaders, volunteers, and mentors who have poured into our children's lives. Your love and sacrifice have made a lasting impact on them. I'm also thankful for the years I spent with students, learning so much about myself, leadership, and fully relying on God.

Being part of the worship team has brought some of my deepest memories. We've lived a lot of life together — hard years, beautiful years, tears, laughter, and everything in between. I'm thankful I was able to contribute to the recordings during the pandemic, sharing our church with people who couldn't physically attend.

Thank you, Church Project, for the years of life we've shared. You have strengthened, comforted, refined, and shaped us into who we are today. I know there is so much more to come, and I look forward to the years of growth, transformation, and community ahead. Happy birthday, CP! Thank you, Jason and Brooke, for everything you've done to make this church what it is.

BJ & LINDSAY MUNSON

THREE

Ministry Partners

We serve our city through Ministry Partners. We partner with world changing organizations locally and globally that do good and share the gospel. We also join our lives together to serve alongside others in the work.

Since the beginning of Church Project, our people have been dedicated to meet needs in our city.

We have started a free and charitable urgent care clinic for the uninsured and underinsured in our city.

We have taken action together for local, national and global disasters by mobilizing ourselves to serve physically, by partnering with local ministries and relief organizations, and by giving financially to meet needs.

We have led the way in serving under-resourced families with the largest back to school outreach in our city. We have been a host church for Night to Shine in multiple years.

We have deployed ourselves to give of our time in regular rhythms where our people are serving alongside Ministry Partners to serve the most vulnerable in our city – orphans, widows, survivors of human trafficking, ex-offenders, homeless, and more.

And our work isn't over. Imagine if more prisoners were spurred on by Christ's love as they re-enter society. More sex trafficking survivors realized their identity in God and were redeemed by His grace. More under-resourced families in our city were served and more of our city's homeless population met with kindness and generosity. More refugees and immigrants were welcomed and thriving in House Churches across our city.

Together, we can support local ministries in greater ways in the coming year – with increased financial giving, with every person in Church Project serving regularly, and with new Ministry Partners doing good in our city.

These are stories of how God has used Church Project to meet real needs in our city and world by partnering with Ministry Partners to share the love and generosity of Christ.

———————

About 11 years ago, I got a call from a friend asking if I wanted to join her to feed the homeless. I instantly said yes, picturing a cafeteria setting where I'd serve food with a big spoon. When we arrived, it was just someone's house. Dave Droll opened the door, and we went in to cook and pray. Afterward, we loaded into trucks and headed out to feed the homeless on the freeway. At our first stop, people came to the vehicle, and we served them a hot meal, learned their names, shook hands, and prayed with them. I felt blessed but guilty, seeing how much I had compared to what they had.

There was a song at that time with the lyric, *Break my heart for what breaks yours.* I sincerely asked God to break my heart for what breaks His, and He did. I became heartbroken for the homeless, the broken, and the abandoned. The following Saturday, I served again and began remembering names and faces. I realized that Jesus would walk with the hungry, the needy, and the homeless, and everyone has a unique story.

I used to judge the homeless, thinking they made bad choices, but I learned they aren't all irresponsible addicts. Many are broken-hearted people, and I began to see them through the eyes of Jesus. There needs to be more help, and people depend on the ministry. They know the trucks, the honks, and the stops. If we don't show up, we break their trust. It's not just about serving to check a box; it's about truly caring.

Serving fills me and makes me want to share that blessing with others. Seeing lives change through love and action would be amazing.

NANCY FRASIER, HOPE BEYOND BRIDGES

I first learned about Houston Welcomes Refugees (HWR) at Church

Project a few months after moving to The Woodlands. The mission of HWR — to create friendship bonds with refugees leading to good-God-gospel conversations — spoke deeply to me, and I knew God was calling me to be a part of it. I joined a Welcome Team and discovered the family I was connecting with lived just 5 minutes from my old house.

I struggled with frustration, questioning why God moved us. I felt I could do so much more for the family back in my old neighborhood. I vented to God: *Why did you take me away from there? I could be this family's best friend. Why am I here?* God spoke through the Holy Spirit: *Yes, maybe YOU could do more there, but I AM. I, the Lord God, am the one who saves. You are called to be my hands and feet.*

Praise God for revealing Himself to me! How often do I try to be the savior instead of pointing to the Savior? God showed me that He is the righteous one and the Savior — my only job is to point to Him.

MADELINE NISSEN

Debs: We are Josh and Debs Walker from Dublin, Ireland. We came to the U.S. 13 years ago as missionaries, knowing God had called us here. The transition was a shock — though we expected similarities, the cultural differences were profound. We started volunteering in Houston's inner city, where I was serving food when I saw a small baby left alone in the parking lot. That moment broke my heart and sparked a journey focused on people who lack both a Heavenly Father and an earthly father.

Josh: We realized that cycles of poverty often start with fatherless families, creating a fatherless generation. 7MORE embodies Jesus' teaching on forgiveness — 70 times seven isn't a number but a mindset of not counting the past, instead seeing people for their potential and how God sees them.

Debs: Our broken hearts now long to help those stuck in these cycles. As we've gone to the bus stop, we've met people in similar situations, and we feel deeply called to be part of their healing. A broken heart for people is what drives us.

JOSH & DEBS WALKER, 7MORE

At 17, I was sex trafficked and moved through several abusive foster homes. My case manager left me on the side of the road after I got kicked out of a foster home, and the police had to intervene. I was constantly fighting and felt hopeless, like nobody loved me. Every day felt like it could be my last. After going to jail, I truly believed it saved my life. I prayed for a way out of the trafficking, drugs, and streets. I knew Christ loved me, but I struggled with the idea that He could forgive all I'd done.

In jail, I prayed for God to save me from myself, and He truly did. Since being out, I've been coming to Church Project for about five months. God blessed me with a safe home and surrounded me with safe people. I've been given a new opportunity for a new life. Pastor Jason's constant message to *just do the next right thing* has stuck with me. I don't want to do the wrong thing anymore. It feels good, and I know it encourages others around me as well. I often think about where I could be if I hadn't given my life to Christ. The small things He's done in my life are amazing, and I now know He truly accepted me.

MADISON, REDEEMED MINISTRIES

We will be married 26 years this year. Our first time out with South Route, we had almost 40 people that we served. It was a good experience, and it felt like this was a ministry we could be a part of. We brought our kids with us for years. We had to remember to see people with the eyes of Christ — not to judge by their clothes, but to focus on their hearts and let them see Christ in us.

I used to prejudge people on the street, always thinking they were just out there to get money, without knowing anything about their personal story. I was quick to judge. But once we started serving, it changed my perspective. Now, when I see people — not just on Saturdays when we're serving with Hope Beyond Bridges — but any time, I see them as people, as God's creation, not as someone trying to scam others.

JOHN FOREMAN, HOPE BEYOND BRIDGES

I was the first female in my family to leave New Hampshire and enlist in the Marine Corps. It sounded exciting — traveling and doing cool things. I was successful until an incident that left me surrounded by men who didn't want a female Marine. At 18 or 19, I couldn't handle the trauma I experienced. I felt hopeless and thought no one would want me, a broken, trauma-filled young woman. I ended up marrying my military abuser.

Growing up Roman Catholic, I didn't understand God or the value of a relationship with Him. But when I found the church, it opened my eyes to a new way of worshiping and walking in the image of Christ. If it weren't for those experiences, I couldn't help others now.

During the pandemic, I took a leap of faith and left my part-time job to start a nonprofit for veterans. As a woman veteran, single mom, and Christ follower, I saw the need for mental health peer support in Montgomery County and Texas. So, I created the Institute for Peer Support, helping veterans stabilize and get the help they need.

Through this, I've been able to give back what I've received — spiritually, mentally, emotionally, and physically — by coming alongside others. God has blessed me with the opportunity to pay it forward. In Him, I found the confidence to share my story and trust that everything would be okay.

JENNIFER CANNON, VETERANS SUPPORT

As a kid, I loved marbles. My friends and I would play in the streets, as that was our only form of entertainment. The Taliban controlled Afghanistan at the time, and we had no TV or music because they prohibited them. They tracked houses with antennas, and punishments for violating their rules were severe — physical punishment or imprisonment. We weren't allowed to shout, make calls, or even seek help.

One night, during a mission, our vehicle was caught in an ambush for about 40-45 minutes between insurgents and the Swedish army. I was the only one left in the vehicle while the soldiers engaged in the fight. It felt like I was all alone. Then, silence followed, and I thought everyone had been killed. But I heard the sound of a helicopter, and a light shone on my car. When I saw them, I was overjoyed. It felt like someone was finally coming for me.

I was welcomed by 20 people, and their warmth surprised me. I'm forever thankful for them. When I showed pictures to my parents, they were amazed at how I was treated like family. The support from that team made me feel like I wasn't alone. My parents were so happy, and it was a moment of true relief and connection.

AN AFGHAN REFUGEE, HOUSTON WELCOMES REFUGEES

The night of the storm, we saw it coming. Lights were going out every-where, and I had a bad feeling it might take longer than expected. I was called into work that day, so I drove down 290, passing cops, knowing the winds were doing damage. Every now and then, I'd see the blue flashes from downed power lines. There was pure destruction everywhere — poles inside homes, trees in living rooms.

Multiple guys from my House Church reached out, offering help since I was working late hours. Just seeing those messages reminded me that some-one always has your back when you're plugged into a House Church. As soon as the storm hit, people sent out prayer requests and updates, offering food, shelter, and help. It was an overwhelming outpouring of love.

After the storm, I realized that, just like the customers I served, I wanted answers. I was working hard, but I had to trust and be still. Reflecting later, I realized this is how it works — sometimes we don't have all the answers, but we keep trusting. And in those moments, people take notice and start asking about the church you attend. It sparks something, and I try to fan that flame.

A LINEMAN, SERVICING OUR CITY
AFTER THE APRIL 2024 FLOODS

I was in a terrible place because I'd never had to ask for help. My daugh-ter made bad decisions, and her kids were taken by the system in another state. It drained nearly all our savings to get my grandkids home. I prayed for a solution, and that's when the Garden Adult Item called my mother about a lady who helped set us up. That's when we found Angel Reach, and I've seen God work through them ever since.

For 11 years, Angel Reach has helped our family without asking ques-tions. When my husband got cancer, they provided an oxygen machine and a scooter so he could get around. Without them, my grandkids would never have had Christmas or Easter. Every year, Angel Reach has provided Christmas gifts, school clothes, and supplies for my grandkids. I can't imag-ine what we'd do without them. Their care means the world to me.

DEBBIE ZANN, ANGEL REACH

On May 12th, 2017, the night before Mother's Day, I tucked my kids into bed, gave them hugs, and went to sleep. Around 3 a.m., I noticed the kitchen light was off, which was unusual. When I got up, I smelled smoke and started banging on the walls. My parents had already called 911. The stairs were burning, and I couldn't get through to my kids. I kept shouting, *My babies!*

That's when my dad jumped out of the second story window, grabbed a ladder, and helped me get to safety. I prayed, asking God not to take my kids, but if He had to, to let me walk away. And He answered. My brother came down, burned, and my dad followed. I felt overwhelmed by God's mercy.

I used to be upset when people didn't know what to say, but I realized they just didn't know how to help. I often felt lonely, wondering why God allowed such suffering. But now I see that everything has a purpose. If it weren't for that fire, I wouldn't be the person I am today.

Two days later, on Mother's Day, I was in my room crying when my son came in with roses, a card, and a teddy bear, saying, *Happy Mother's Day.* It meant so much. With God, we can overcome anything. If it weren't for Him, I don't know where I'd be.

MOTHER FROM A FAMILY HELPED AFTER
GREAT LOSS FROM A HOUSEFIRE

Todd: We saw a video of a man recently released from prison, and it really struck a chord with us. Sadie and I decided to contact them and find out how we could get involved.

Sadie: When I learned more about the ministry, I told Todd, *We need to pray about this.* He was on board immediately. That was about two years ago.

Todd: A lot of these men and women come out of prison with anxiety, unsure about how their families will react, how society will view them, or what they'll do next. Reconnecting with family, who may have been falling apart while they were in prison, is also a huge challenge. So, for them to come out and see a loving face — someone who doesn't condemn them, but just wants to help — is something they really appreciate. They vocalize that often.

Sadie: Debs asked if I would be okay in this environment, and I told her a bit about my story before coming to Christ — how I was an addict for many years and even homeless for a time. When we got there, it was a tough day. My heart broke for the people, and there was a lot of heaviness.

Todd: One gentleman had been in prison for 47 years. When I offered him a phone to call his family, he couldn't even understand how to use it. I dialed the number for him. He spoke a lot about the Lord, but I wasn't sure he truly understood what it meant to be a follower of Christ. So, I went over and talked with him about the Lord, and he gave his life to Christ.

Sadie: It was a great opportunity to practice walking in obedience, to love people we don't know, and to get out of our comfort zones to do the work God has for us. It doesn't take much time, just a few hours here and there, but those simple acts mean a lot.

TODD & SADIE ARMSTREET, 7MORE

I've been living in the USA for eight years. We moved from Reynosa, Mexico, when my husband was transferred to Houston for work. It was hard at first, especially going to the grocery store, trying to find someone who looked familiar, like a Hispanic face. I was ashamed to speak English, afraid people would laugh at me. But we started attending a nearby House Church, and my kids loved the summer camp. We were drawn to how the church taught the Bible verse by verse, just like we did in Spanish growing up.

One day, I saw an email about a need for ESL teachers. I thought, *I'm not a teacher, but I want to be a student.* So, I joined the English classes. Over time, I stopped worrying about my English. The people at the House Church were patient and loving. They gave their time to help me, and through the classes, I felt Jesus' presence everywhere.

Being able to speak English and share about Jesus in English has been a miracle. It's the best thing, and I'm so grateful for the opportunity to build relationships and serve.

NADIA PADILLA, ENGLISH CLASSES

In 2016, we moved into the big red barn on 1488, and it became an iconic home for Mercy House. It was where ministry flowed out of, and what started with just Chris and me became a team of people doing ministry together. We have ties with refugees from Russian-speaking countries, so we invited friends working in Ukraine to our barn. We were raising money for helmets, bulletproof vests, and supplies for people evacuated to bomb shelters in Ukraine.

During a meeting, as our friend explained the need for helmets, the floor suddenly dropped six inches, like a roller coaster. We didn't even think, we just prayed. It was a powerful moment, and Yvonne said, *Do you still wonder why you need helmets?* If this floor had collapsed, we would've needed them. But in Ukraine, they face concrete buildings collapsing.

Five minutes later, we went live, and God showed up. After evacuating the building, structural engineers told us it was unsafe. That night, we reached out to Jason Shepperd, who immediately offered a new space for us. We moved 7,000 square feet of warehousing, an online store, and even set up a studio. The Church Project family has been extremely gracious. Over the years, the floor has figuratively fallen beneath us many times, but when you step into the crisis of the world, the enemy tries to stop the gospel. But because of the generosity of this church, we didn't miss a beat—we sent out 3,000 boxes the next day.

When I say Church Project has come alongside us, I mean you, the church family. You have made a difference in ministry, and mercy has come.

KRISTEN WELCH, MERCY HOUSE GLOBAL

I'll never forget one student whose apartment caught on fire. She and her single mom lost everything. The only clothes she had were on her back, and she had no shoes. They came to school crying, and I felt so bad for them. I bought her a backpack and shoes because they couldn't afford them.

I went to the booth one day, not knowing much about the back-to-school ministry. The coordinator said, *I'm looking for someone to take over this ministry.* I was nervous, having never been involved before, but I met with the counselors. I learned that parents always looked forward to receiving backpacks, and how something as simple as a haircut, new shoes, or new clothes could boost a child's confidence.

What started as providing school supplies has now grown to include uniforms, shoes, haircuts, food, and supplies. It's amazing how much this ministry has expanded. It's all God's work. I've seen that it takes all of us to make a difference. As they say, *It takes a village to raise a child*, and the same is true here. Every small part contributes to a bigger impact.

SHERYL ALVAREZ, BACK TO SCHOOL BETTER

I've been here, local, about 47 years and have chronic lymphocytic leukemia. For ten years, I've needed blood transfusions. When I was in the hospital, I had to take expensive medication, but Medicare helped lower the cost to $2,700 a month, which is still a lot for me. When I came home, I was sick and unsure what to do. I prayed, and God told me, *Be still, let me be who I am.* Soon after, my niece called and said people from Church Project were coming to help.

I didn't expect much, but they kept coming and working, even though the pipes kept breaking. They said they couldn't leave me like this and arranged for a crew from California, certified plumbers, to come assess and fix everything. I was speechless. Then a lady from Church Project came to my door with dinner. She said, *I'm from Church Project,* and I couldn't believe it. The love, joy, and service I experienced from them were beyond anything I expected. I heard them singing and worshiping God, and their love never stopped. It's something that's stuck with me ever since.

HOMEOWNER HELPED IN 2021 WINTER FREEZE

I was trafficked in strip clubs, on the streets, on the internet, and in casinos. Everywhere I went, people would approach me and try to minister to me, but I'd cuss them out. I would ask, *If there's a God, where is He? Why did this happen to me as a little girl? Why would He let this happen if He loves me?*

One day, I met a woman who shared the gospel with me in a way I'd never heard before. She had been through the same struggles and told me that even when I questioned God, He was always there, loving me. As she spoke, memories flooded back of times God had chased after me. There was no denying Him anymore. I fell to my knees and accepted Him into my heart.

When she came to the house, she was timid and unsure, struggling with the curriculum. She faced difficult topics that made her want to run. Redeem was harder than what she'd been through because she had to face the pain and heal, something she'd spent her whole life avoiding.

After two years in the house, she knew what she wanted for her future. Now, she's living her dream as a hairstylist. Watching her journey with the Lord has been incredible, and seeing her joy grow is amazing. I'm so grateful for the people who didn't give up on me and kept loving me, even when I pushed them away.

At Redeemed, we see Jesus show up every day. He's given us hope, sustainability, and answers, and there's no other reason for that except Jesus. As a church, we need to rise up and speak to our families about human trafficking. It's happening in our communities, and we must equip ourselves to be part of the solution. God calls us to rise, learn, and go.

AMANDA, REDEEMED MINISTRIES

FOUR

Network

We are a Network of Churches. Through Church Project Network, we plant churches not for the sake of growth, but to ensure the health and sustainability of the Church. In the past four years, over 40,000 churches in the U.S. have closed, with many more at risk. This demands our attention. We must plant more healthy churches.

God has been faithful to our mission, and we've seen His hand in the growth and strengthening of Church Project Network. For this vision to flourish, continued investment — both spiritually and financially — is necessary to equip leaders, plant churches, and create sustainable, decentralized discipleship communities committed to spreading the gospel.

Additionally, we partner with like-minded churches who share in a pursuit of becoming a *Church of House Churches*. By hosting regional conferences, coaching cohorts, and offering targeted training, we are not just planting churches — we are fostering vibrant communities that reflect the New Testament model of church. These partnerships help plant churches and encourage existing communities to thrive in the mission of making disciples.

Looking ahead, Church Project Network will need to multiply more leaders, expand globally, and raise healthier, more effective churches. As we rely on God's faithfulness, we remain committed to building a network that will make a lasting impact on the Kingdom of God by planting churches that bring the gospel to new places and people with new contexts and cultures. We support new Church Projects locally and globally through leadership vetting, culture training, building procurement, and more, with each Church Project rethinking and returning to a New Testament ecclesiology.

These are stories from Church Project Network and the men and women who are planting and growing *Churches of House Churches.*

When we moved back to The Woodlands in 2010, we began searching for a church that was theologically sound, culturally relevant, and dedicated to helping people develop a closer relationship with Christ.

We wanted a church where we could grow, be spiritually challenged, and assist others in doing the same. We sought a church with a strong Pastor, preacher, and leader.

Church Project was one of the first churches we attended, and we quickly became convinced that this church met all our criteria.

We quickly became engaged in House Church and began leading a House Church, which birthed additional House Churches, and that is still producing even more House Churches 15 years later. We started sharing our lives with the people we met in those House Churches, who have since become lifelong friends.

Church Project has inspired and challenged us to live out our faith in the everyday moments of our everyday relationships, from family to friends to the waiters and waitresses who serve us our food. Church Project has reminded us and challenged us to stay faithful to timeless biblical truth in the face of culture influencing a worldview where truth is relative. Church Project has provided a context where we can use our gifts to serve the people inside and outside the four walls of our church. Church Project has inspired us to be radically generous with everything God has supplied us. Church Project has been a tangible example of God building his church and inspired me to dream big and ask God to do big things in my life and personal ministry.

It is both humbling and a privilege to call Church Project my home and to play a small role in leading a worldwide movement that influences and plants other churches, changing how people see Christ, Christians, and the Church. As much as God has done over the past 15 years in the life of Church Project, I genuinely believe that our greatest days of influence are ahead.

HANS MOLEGRAAF, ELDER

My family and I began attending Church Project in January of 2014. I had served in local church ministry for twelve years and was tired and disenchanted with much of the church culture I had experienced. My family needed a healthy place where we could heal, grow, and gain clarity on what God wanted us to do next. We immediately got into a House Church where we found rich and authentic community with people we loved deeply, and still do to this day. We found healing for our souls and direction for our lives from the teaching of the word. God began to make clear his desire for us. Over the course of that year our hearts and God's timing began to align, and it became clear that he was leading us to help plant a new Church Project.

In 2015 we moved to Conroe, joined the only House Church there, and soon became hosts to the second one, all while planning, preparing, and praying for what God was about to do. These two Conroe House Churches became the beginning of a new Church Project that began collecting a core of people in 2016. We found space at the Outlets of Conroe where we could gather and began renovations late that year. March 5, 2017 we launched our first Sunday Gathering and fourth House Church.

Since that day God has continued to show himself faithful as we remain committed to this relentless pursuit of being the church he originally intended for us to be. *A Church of House Churches*, gathering in ways that reflect the New Testament Church, cultivating radical generosity for the sake of Jesus' name in our city. Today we have fifteen House Churches, more than five hundred people gathering regularly, and a dozen ministries that we have partnered with for the sake of the Gospel in our city and our world.

Watching our marriage, our four daughters, our friends, and our church grow for these past eight years has been the greatest joy of my life. The work of Pastoring people has been a gift from God that I treasure. Watching people come to know Jesus, be folded into Biblical Community, and Serve our city has brought so much joy.

I am thankful to be a part of the story of Church Project. The last fifteen years have lead to a lot of incredible things. I can't wait to see what God has in store for the future of this church, this network, this movement. All for the praise and glory of Jesus alone!

MATT RULE, CP NORTH COUNTY LEAD PASTOR

In the past year Church Project Orange County has gathered in three different locations and continued to meet in homes as House Churches across our community. We have said goodbye to a number of faithful and committed families who have been part of what right now seems like a steady migration from California. However, as we approach the end of another year we can look back and see the Lord's kindness and faithfulness to us.

We have seen the Lord provide for our ongoing location needs, and despite the many challenges have been able to meet every Sunday morning as a gathering of God's people who love Jesus, love each other, and love to follow Jesus' mission in this world. We have seen new believers take their first steps in following Jesus by being baptized and joining House Churches. We've seen children and others who have followed Jesus for longer be baptized too. We've seen families being ministered to in their House Churches, having needs met and experiencing the kindness and generosity of the Lord through the hands and feet of His people. We've heard stories from people in these House Churches about how they are reaching out to neighbors and friends, and sensing God at work in those conversations. We've also seen people change as they have stepped into these more intimate discipleship communities for the first time and experienced love, encouragement, and friendship – often for the first time in a long time.

This year we sent our first family on full-time mission to help introduce people in Tanzania to Jesus through the work of Bible translation. In doing so we have been able to deepen our engagement with ministry partners in Jerusalem (literally), Judea, and the ends of the earth. Working with local ministry partners, we have formed Caring Communities to provide wrap around care for families within and outside our church who are in the challenging world of foster care and adoption. We have also provided immediate safety, shelter, and sanctuary for families experiencing acute crisis.

Since our launch just over six years ago, by the pursuit of simplicity for the sake of generosity we have built up reserves from which we have been able to respond to disaster relief nationally, but also to people's personal 'disasters' locally. We are grateful for the ongoing generosity of the Lord's people in our church family, and their desire to give of their time, talents, and resources as part of their walk with Jesus.

As we roll towards a new year, our future location needs continue to be on our hearts and minds. As a church we have lived a nomadic life in terms of our Gathering Space. We are very thankful for all the spaces that the Lord has provided us to use but it would be nice to have somewhere to call *home*, at least for a while. As the Lord brings our small church family to mind, we'd appreciate your prayers for that. Also, the ongoing loss of good people is hard. We have said some tearful goodbyes, and there are more to come. However, there has also been the joy of meeting and greeting new visitors who have stuck around and begun to step in and step up. Perhaps this comment from one of our church family expresses it best.

I've been attending Church Project for over a year and so thankful God led me to this intergenerational congregation of people who want to know God and live for Him.

Thank you Church Project and the Church Project Network for your ongoing support, wisdom and encouragement. God is good. He is who He says He is. He knows what He is doing. We have much to be thankful for!
BRIAN WILSON, CP ORANGE COUNTY LEAD PASTOR

We attended CP in 2015 after being invited to First Wednesday by a coworker. We got plugged into a House Church where we were exposed to diverse community for the first time. We also participated in biblical meditation for the first time which impacted our walk with the Lord. We went on a mission trip and saw God work in and through the participants. We were devastated to leave CP when Daniel's job moved us to north Texas. Fast forward 8 years, and God presented an opportunity to plant Church Project Van Alstyne. The longing of our hearts was to be at Church Project, but also to raise our family in Van Alstyne. He is so good to have provided both. Thanks to CP and the House Church model, 100 residents of Van Alstyne have been plugged into community and are studying the scriptures together on Sunday mornings and in House Church, many of whom were not in church prior to CPVA. Praise God for the vision of CP 15 years ago, what it has meant to us, and what it will grow to mean to so many in the future. The gospel is going forth!

LAUREN HINSON, CP VAN ALSTYNE FOUNDER

Congratulations, Church Project on 15 years of faithful obedience and witness to God's call in pursuing His design for His Church! God has not only built Church Project, but has expanded His kingdom here on earth through the intentional gospel work of planting Churches of House Churches through Church Project Network.

For the past two years, we have had the privilege of being equipped, encouraged, and supported through Church Project Network to plant Church Project River Valley in Central Arkansas. We are experiencing the joy of seeing lives changed as we engage in good, God, gospel conversations, as well as biblical community being deeply cultivated through our House Churches.

In the hardship and difficulties we've experienced on this journey thus far, the support of Church Project and the encouragement received through our monthly Church Project Network cohort have been a grace of God that has sustained us and helped us persevere for the glory of God. Without Church Project coming alongside us, we would have given up early on and missed out on the blessing of walking in obedience and seeing God do what only He can do.

We are hopeful and excited about the days ahead, not just for Church Project River Valley but for all the Church Project family and network of churches around the world.

Our cities and world need a biblical expression and model of who God intended the Church to be for the sake of making much of Christ and gospel proclamation. We believe God has raised up and positioned Church Project, and the network of CP churches, to continue carrying out the mission of Christ until the day of Christ.

As the apostle Paul said to the believers in Colossae, *We give thanks to God, the Father of our Lord Jesus Christ, praying always for you*, Church Project.

SHAWN BARNARD, CP RIVER VALLEY LEAD PASTOR

CP has been a tremendous source of strength and support for me and my family as we've journeyed in our surrender to Jesus. Without the faithful prayers, sacrificial generosity, and ongoing spiritual care we would not have been in a place to plant, shepherd, and steward CP Tomball.

Thank you CP for being the all that God has called you to be to our city!

BILLY SCHIEL, CP TOMBALL LEAD PASTOR

In January 2010, I was on train in Europe with my then boss who floated the idea of a work move to Houston, Texas. Little did we know as our family prayed, journaled and sought guidance on such a significant move, that a small group of like minded believers were gathering in a location a few miles from our soon to be home. On arrival in The Woodlands in August 2010, our family quickly found our way to CP thanks to an invite from the Cheesemans (a Scottish couple who were already connected into life at CP!). God quickly made it clear to us that he had used my work relocation for a much bigger purpose than my career.

As I look back on our own imminent 15 year anniversary of life in USA, our story is inextricably linked to life at CP. Life in Texas for the Booths would look a lot different had we not stumbled into that dark warehouse on Timberloch 14.5 years ago. The friendships forged, the teachings heard, the worship shared, and the community built, have been our strength and stay through the highs and lows of ex-pat life. As it relates to CP, I always thought of Project to mean *work in progress* but on the night that CP North County was launched, my parents were visiting and my Latin *speaking* dad casually said *project* is a great name for a church because it means to *throw forward* and that's what you guys are doing with church planting!

It's great to look back and see God's faithfulness, but as we look back on 15 incredible years, we remain in *throw forward* mode as, under Jason's fearless leadership, supported by an incredible staff and volunteer infrastructure, we look to press on in to all that God has called Church Project to do and be. Much has been achieved for the kingdom in 15 fast years, but there is much still to be done, all for His glory and purposes. Vamos!

GEORGE BOOTH, ELDER

When I first encountered Church Project, I was focused on improving the small groups within the church I was pastoring. My goal was simple — make them more effective. But as I learned about CP's ecclesiology, I was captivated by something deeper. It wasn't just what CP believes; it was how those beliefs are put into action.

One particular story stood out to me: a CP House Church stepped in to support a woman whose house had burned down. The church didn't just sympathize from afar; they actively cared for her in her time of need. I thought to myself, *I wish my small groups could be this proactive, this hands-on in loving not only our brothers and sisters in Christ but also our neighbors.*

As I was mentored by CP staff, the churches we planted in Mexico began to implement what we had learned about how the early church made disciples and cared for one another. The results were profound. Not only did our own congregations thrive, but other churches in Latin America began to take notice of our growing, multiplying church model. They wanted to know what we were doing differently.

Today, Church Project is helping Pastors all over the world rethink and return to a more biblical approach to church life. It's inspiring to see how churches are being transformed, aligning more closely with the vision Christ intended for His church. We are deeply grateful for Church Project's unwavering commitment to this vision, and it's a privilege to be part of a movement that is changing the way people see Christ, Christians and the church around the globe.

PABLO DI GILIO, CP MIAMI LEAD PASTOR
& NETWORK DIRECTOR

Jason & Brooke Shepperd assembling chairs, Timberloch Pl, January 10, 2010

Sunday Gathering, Pruitt Rd, 2024

Church Project Interest Meeting, 2010

2407 Timberloch Pl (Warehouse), 2010-2014

295 Sawdust Rd (Old Kroger), 2014-2020

602 Pruitt Rd (Old Legends Sports Complex), 2020-Present

Sunday Gathering, Timberloch Pl, 2011

Unpacking chairs, Sawdust Rd, 2014

Sunday Gathering, 295 Sawdust Rd, 2015

Sunday Gathering, 602 Pruitt Rd, 2023

Sunday Gathering, Sawdust Rd, 2018

Online Gathering, Jason Shepperd & Dave Edwards, 2023

Sunday Gathering, Wes Arvin & Stephanie Harris, Timberloch Pl, 2011

First Wednesday, Pruitt Rd, 2023

Baptisms, Katherine Henderson & Jason Shepperd, Timberloch Pl, 2011

Baptisms, Hans & Calvin Molegraaf, Sawdust Rd, 2015

Baptisms, Calvin Taylor & Jake Petefish, Sawdust Rd, 2018

Baptisms, Sean Kennard, Ryan Garner & Graham Dodson, Pruitt Rd, 2024

Sunday Gathering, Timberloch Pl, 2011

Sunday Gathering, Sawdust Rd, 2015

Sunday Gathering, Timberloch Pl, 2011

Sunday Gathering, Pruitt Rd, 2023

First Wednesday, Jason Shepperd, Pruitt Rd, 2022

First Wednesday, Pruitt Rd, 2024

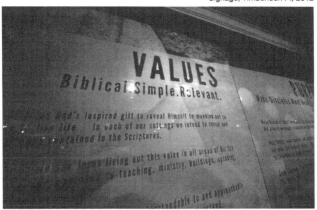

Signage, Timberloch Pl, 2012

Sunday Gathering Communication, 2019

Sunday Gathering, Sawdust Rd, 2019

The Wade Family, Sawdust Rd, 2015

Project KIDS, Sawdust Rd, 2015

Project KIDS, Kid Camp, 2024

FIFTY6, Timberloch Pl, 2013

FIFTY6, Retreat, 2024

Project STUDENTS, Encounter, 2013

Project STUDENTS, Encounter, 2024

House Church Wall, Sawdust Rd, 2017

House Church Wall, Pruitt Rd, 2023

House Church, 2022

Spanish House Church, December 2010

Spanish House Church, May 2011

Belize Global Trip, 2024

Disaster Response, 2018

Good City Health, 2024

Back to School Better, August 2024

Night to Shine, February 2024

House Church Training, Tajikistan, 2024

House Church Training, Nepal, 2024

CP Puebla, Mexico, 2024

CP Haiti, 2018

2:47pm Prayer, 2024

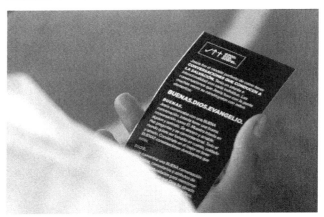

GOOD.GOD.GOSPEL., Guatemala, 2024

FIVE

Evangelism

Everyone can be an evangelist. This is at the heart of why we pray daily at 2:47pm, why we have Good.God.Gospel. conversations, and why we have created tools like our gospel icons.

We have seen God move powerfully in our city and around the world through conversations that lead to salvation. Our approach to evangelism is simple: everyone is an evangelist. And its modeled after the way Jesus had conversations with people. To equip our church and others, we created Good.God.Gospel. – a resource designed to help guide conversations that can naturally turn good conversations to God conversations, and ultimately to gospel conversations.

We created 8 simple icons with key words, descriptions, and Bible verses that communicate the powerful gospel of Jesus in a way that can be communicated without common language, just through the use of visual symbols.

And we developed the Good.God.Gospel. app, making it accessible to anyone, anywhere, at any time. God's faithfulness has been evident as we continue translating this tool into more and more languages and adapt this tool further for kids and students, empowering the next generation to share the gospel as well.

God has been faithful to bless these efforts and is using our church to love our city. This tool has transformed how our church shares the good news of Jesus, and we have seen many in our community use it to lead

people to Christ. Other churches and ministries are leveraging Good.God.
Gospel. to better share the gospel too.

We pray daily at 2:47pm for those we want to see God save, for ourselves to be prepared and given opportunities for conversations and for our
church to be bold in sharing the gospel and praying for our city.

And throughout the year, we celebrate baptisms in homes, through
House Church and in Sunday Gatherings.

As we move forward, we are committed to continuing this work of
evangelism, both here and around the world. We will keep sharing the
gospel through Good.God.Gospel. conversations and praying for those who
are still far from God.

These are stories of salvation and of how God has used Church Project
to impact lives with the gospel. These stories fuel our faith and remind us of
God's relentless love for the lost.

I am the granddaughter of a sharecropper, and we lived on the land
without cold or hot water, but we got by. My grandparents were believers, and I thought I was too, but I didn't fully understand faith at that time.
When I was 14, we got a phone call while on our way to church, and I could
hear my grandmother saying, *It's going to be okay.* Later, we came back to get
a second call. I heard her scream, and I knew something bad had happened.
My sister had been shot by her husband and bled out before help could
arrive. That was a hard thing for me to comprehend.

When I was 18, my brother was killed by gang members over a jacket
he wouldn't give up. I don't even remember his funeral, just feeling cold.
That's when the anger started building up. I became very guarded, hitting
people for no reason, and refusing to trust anyone. I told myself I was the
only one in control and that no one would get close.

It took an incident at the hospital to bring all that pain to the forefront.
I shared everything with CP Prayer, and my House Church came alongside
me. They were there for me, asking what they could do to help — and they
followed through. They didn't turn their backs on me. I realized that I still
had unforgiveness in my heart, things I thought I had worked through but

hadn't. God showed me that even a little unforgiveness in His sight is not forgiveness at all. I had to give it all to Him.

It was a freeing moment, like my soul was set free. The goodness of God was displayed in the people around me, and accepting their love was like accepting God's love for me. It was God saying, *I will send My people into your life to show you the love I have for you through them.* It reminded me that, when you ask someone how they're doing, you never know what they might be going through. Many people believe but have been hurt. I always tell them, *Everybody's broken, but God will send someone to show you His love. In the end, God is good.*

BEV BROWN

Growing up with my mom as a single mother, we couldn't afford day-care, so she told me to stay home after school and lock the doors until she got back. I didn't always follow that rule, spending my time with friends, living life as I saw fit. This continued into my 30s, even after getting married and starting a family. I tried to balance my partying lifestyle with being a husband and father, but I could always pull it off — partying until 3:30 AM and still getting up for work at 7:30. When I drank, I became a character I created — Graham, the life of the party. But the fun always ended when I was alone.

My wife encouraged me to go to church, and I eventually got baptized. I thought, *Now what? You're supposed to fix all my problems.* But I still felt empty. I prayed for things, but nothing changed. I got angry with God, feeling like I was doing everything right, but He wasn't answering me. That's when I hit rock bottom and decided to destroy everything I had.

Then, at 42, while training in jujitsu, I felt a sharp pain in my back and couldn't move. I went into convulsions and ended up in the hospital. I was told I had a heart attack and 95% blockage in my *widow maker.* I had to go into surgery immediately. As they prepped me, I realized my life was flashing before my eyes, and I wasn't happy with what I saw. I said my first real prayer, asking for God's help.

After surgery, the doctor told me it was a normal heart attack — nothing I had done caused it. But it hit me hard. With all the medications and a stent in place, I had to stop drinking. That's when I decided to finally submit to God. It wasn't easy, but once I accepted His grace, He began to rebuild me into someone I never thought I could be. Now, I want to share that with others: it's not hard to break free. Jesus has already overcome it.

GRAHAM DODSON

I grew up going to church every Sunday and Wednesday, eventually playing drums at church events. I wanted to do full-time ministry and pursued a degree in Biblical Studies. However, there was no emphasis on personal relationship or discipleship — just arguments about who was right. Frustrated, I turned away from God and got into trouble, which led to my arrest for DWI on September 13th, 2019.

At jail, after arguing with a staff member, I was placed on suicide watch. The next morning, a psychiatrist asked me, *What is your will to live?* After wiping my tears away, I said, *To obey God and enjoy Him.* She responded, *I'm a Christian too. Our sin gets us into situations, but we must repent and rely on Him to lead us out.* It felt orchestrated — like God led me to this moment to remind me of my purpose.

When I saw my dad, we both broke down in the car. He said, *This is not who we are.* Through tears, he added, *I didn't realize how much I loved you until this happened.* His words made me reflect on salvation — how we, as guilty sinners, stand before God, justified through faith in Christ, cleansed, renewed, and reconciled.

I began to pray this over and over, and two months later, my lawyer called to say the D.A. had dismissed my case. I've come to a point where everything I have now, I recognize as a product of His grace. And coming to Church, I saw firsthand the embodiment of God's love for us.

IZACK REDMON, CP STAFF

I'm a doer. Show me the goal, and I'll execute. Early on, I was trying to give my sales pitch, trying to win people to Christ, but nobody was coming. I was frustrated — what am I doing wrong? I kept going back to the Word, reading and learning about Jesus, trying to understand how it fit into my life. This was before the internet, so I had to read and dig deep to find answers. Then, I had a revelation: Jesus said, *I will build my church on this.* The gospel itself is the power unto salvation. It's not my job to close the deal, but to engage in relationship and share who Jesus is.

Just the other day, I was dealing with someone at work. I called them up, and at the end, I could tell they were crying. I asked, *Are you okay?* They weren't, and it turned into a 30-minute God conversation. They were Hindu, but I shared the gospel. I didn't see that one coming.

I also serve in a prison release ministry. One time, a prisoner was highly charged, angry, and upset. He was hurt and selling his *wolf tickets*. I prayed, asking God what to do. As I started talking to him, he looked at me and said, *So, you're telling me I need to be nice to this person and do all these things?* I told him, *No, that's not what I'm saying. You can do it for a little while, but eventually, you'll snap and be right back here again.* I explained that nobody can keep the law, but through the Holy Spirit, as you get into the Word and invite Him into your life, what comes out is the change we're talking about.

By the end of our conversation, this man, who had been so aggressive, was as peaceful as a lamb. It was a profound shift. It's not normal to have conversations where people open up like that, where they drop their pretenses and show their true selves. We all hunger to be known and seen. Our response should be immediate. We all respond differently — some of us are cerebral, others passive or aggressive — but the response should be now. Here's the thing: if we're wrong, we've got nothing to lose. But if He is real and He did this for us and we didn't come…wow. The greatest gift and power this world has ever seen has shown itself.

KWASI ENGLISH

My earliest memory is singing Jesus Loves Me next to a piano my mom was playing before I was three. My journey continued at a private Christian school, where the truth of God's Word was challenged by abusive teachers and years of bullying. Through high school and college, life got easier, and I lost my dependence on God. When trials like car accidents and my mom's cancer diagnosis came, I began questioning God. My faith crisis peaked after marrying my husband and moving to Texas, where I had no support system, couldn't find a job, and felt isolated while my husband worked long hours.

Desperately, I started praying to a God I didn't know was still there. Confused by conflicting denominations and teachings, I was unsure what was true. I was raised one way, my husband another, and then I was invited to a Bible study in yet another denomination. For six months, I prayed, searching for God and truth. During one of these Bible studies, surrounded by women, God spoke to me in a personal, undeniable way. In that moment, He showed me that everything I'd experienced was Him working for my good, drawing me into a relationship with Him.

I was undone. Since then, God has seen me through cross-country moves, job losses, the death of my father, 33 years of marriage, and raising three children. The story of my life is a testimony to His goodness and faithfulness. He is everything we need. We can't survive without Him being our bread.

JULIE CHLADNY, HOUSE CHURCH HOST

I was raised in the church with head knowledge of Jesus but lacked a relationship with Him. I was baptized in third grade but thought I needed a radical conversion. This led to a season of rebellion and seeking truth, filled with pride and selfishness. During my long commutes, I used to listen to classic rock, Christian radio, or preachers sharing radical conversion stories. One day, on Highway 105 between College Station and Houston, my eyes were opened to God's truth. I realized how unworthy I was to be in the presence of a holy God. The truth of God's holiness and my sinfulness made me recognize my deep need for a Savior.

Everything I had learned about Jesus, the cross, and His sacrifice became real at that moment. I cried out to God when I got home, knelt on my kitchen floor, and submitted myself to Him. It was a humbling and liberating experience. Through this, God gave me a perfect hope—not wishful thinking, but a godly hope of confident expectation. I now trust that God is who He says He is, that His Word is faithful, and that He is good. All the glory goes to Him.

JON HELANDER

I didn't grow up in a believing home and didn't go to church with my family. At nine, I attended church with a neighbor, but had no real understanding of the Lord. As a teenager, I made choices I regret, and by 20, I was pregnant with my first child. I had two more kids but still had no relationship with the Lord. My three-year-old wanted to go to preschool, so we enrolled her, and I ended up working at the Mother's Day Out at a church. One day, a lady there invited me to church. I said yes, and the following Sunday, I walked into Church Project. I heard the gospel, and after attending for three weeks, I gave my life to the Lord.

The road after hearing the gospel wasn't easy. In fact, it got harder because I now desired to be obedient to God and learn how to live according to His ways. My whole life up until that point had been about self. It was hard to view the world through the lens of the gospel, to die to myself, and to carry my cross daily. I failed many times, learning the same lesson over and over until finally reaching a point of surrender. But it changed me. Each time I chose obedience, my relationship with God grew stronger. Through conflict, trials, and failure, I got closer to Him. Today, I still sit in awe of how God works in my life, caring deeply about the intimate details of my journey. It's amazing.

JENNIFER DEAN, CP STAFF

I'm grateful to have been born into a Christian family in India, but I had a legalistic mentality. I focused on doing the right things daily, believing I could achieve holiness through my works. At 12, during VBS, I learned about Heaven and Hell and followed Christ out of fear, not fully understanding God's grace.

As I grew older and spent more time in the Word, my relationship with Christ deepened. I realized His sacrifice was out of unconditional love for me, and that God's grace couldn't be earned. Building a relationship with God is like any other relationship—you spend time getting to know Him. In His presence, He transforms me into His image and reveals His love.

Now, I can say that Jesus is truth. When I spend time with Him, truth is revealed, and I understand the goodness of God and His faithfulness. I love Him more than ever before.

BEAULAH KONDUR

When I was in youth group, I went to church camps but didn't know why I was there other than I was supposed to show up. My relationships at church felt off, and my relationships with my parents weren't great. In college, I worked in a bar, and when COVID hit, I came home feeling lost.

I tried a couple of churches, but when I visited Church Project, I knew this was it. I met the Browns at the gym, and when they mentioned House Church, I invited myself. Now, they're my people.

In June of last year, my MIMO passed away. I knew it was coming but wasn't ready. Sitting in House Church one day, I felt the need to see her before it was too late. I booked a flight, and when I saw her before she passed, she mentioned going to get her crown and talked about white streets — things that later made sense when I spoke to her Pastor. A month later, Jason's sermon on John 9, about God eternally pursuing us, hit me deeply. Everything changed after that. I dove into my Bible, taking notes and learning.

I sat down with Jen and Josh and told them I wanted to be baptized. They asked, *Ready this Sunday?* and we jumped in the pool together. As an adult, making that decision meant so much more. I'm grateful to be surrounded by people who love me well and remind me of God's love. It's amazing how He places people in your life to show you that love.

FAITH EBERWEIN

I originally wrote a song with a New Age theme: *The New Age has begun.* After coming to the Lord, I rewrote it as *Yes, the Lord has come.* At that time, I didn't know the Lord and had very little humility. I felt in charge of my life and decisions. I traveled a lot, toured Europe with a choir, studied in Vienna, and worked in real estate in Spain. It was exciting and dangerous, and I enjoyed the adventure. But I ventured into drugs, overdid it, and God said, *Okay, you've got to crash now, honey, and then I'll help you.*

After my cocaine addiction, I spent three months in bed, staring at the wall, and finally decided not to kill myself. I chose to keep going and started searching. I got into New Age for eight years—channeling, automatic writing, palm reading. But New Age always promised more, never gave answers. Through a business opportunity, I heard Christian testimonies for the first time. I was disgusted at first, thinking these people were weak, but something changed. I was at a non-denominational church service when I found myself standing up during the altar call. I didn't stand myself up. It was in that moment I realized, *Maybe God has a plan for me. Jesus is what it's all about.*

I was 40 then, and I was thirsty for His word. I began memorizing verses and posting them around my house. I came from a background of fear, and those verses helped me grow strong. I had lived a lifetime of chaos, and it all crashed and burned, but it was necessary to break through my pride. I now know this life is just a small part of something much bigger. We have a glorious future to cling to — the resurrection of Jesus.

AVERY KISER

I was raised in a violent, alcoholic home, full of trauma. I went to church with my mom until I was 13, but then we stopped. As a child, I ran away, and as an adult, I kept running. I worked as a freelancer, often talking with an artist about life and God. He asked me why I didn't believe in God, and I told him it was because I was certain I was going to hell. I never saw God as good. He helped me reimagine God by asking what I'd want God to be, leading me to journal about a loving, kind protector—attributes I never associated with Him.

I moved to Northern California and worked at a fun studio where a woman invited me to her Bible study, which I thought was just a social gathering. I went but always felt out of place, knowing they knew something I didn't. I knew I needed to find a church, so when we moved to Oregon, I asked my husband to help me find one. We found a sweet little home and an amazing church, but I still struggled with accepting Jesus. I spoke with my Pastor, and he encouraged me to read the book of John.

The journey to faith was slow — starting with conversations in Miami, then San Francisco, and finally in Oregon. I prayed for a burning bush but received something deeper: relational connections and the example of people who had faith. Through their patience and love, I finally came to accept Jesus.

AMY NASH

As a police officer, I wanted to make sure my job didn't cost me my wife and future children. So, I started training to become better, eventually becoming a professional MMA fighter. At the time, I was lukewarm—going through the motions without pursuing a real relationship with God or my wife. I worked long hours, and we drifted apart, leading us toward destruction. I was considering divorce when the Lord spoke into my life.

Some godly men poured into me and challenged me. I was looking for an excuse to get a divorce, but they reminded me that it was my responsibility to do the hard work. I realized I had done zero work in my marriage. So, we began putting in real effort, learning the skills to build a strong foundation, rooted in our relationship with God.

I didn't realize how steadfast God was pursuing me, and thankfully, the men in my life helped turn my head to Him. I think it's easier for us to say, *I don't need to give this to the Lord. I can fix this.* There's nothing wrong with accepting the fact that we're broken people and we're not worthy of the gift that the Lord gives us, but Jesus says we're worthy. It's just such a picture of what love actually looks like, and that, I mean, that's how the Lord fights for us. He takes broken things and makes beautiful things out of them.

SEAN KENNARD, HOUSE CHURCH PASTOR

How old am I at 76 and still have a lot of living to go, John? That's how I feel. I was born in Nashville, Tennessee, and raised in beautiful West Virginia. I was married to a military man, and we moved around a lot. I taught preschool for 11 years. My kids used to say, *You play, you don't work.* My parents were Bible scholars, and I wish I knew half of what they knew. I've made many bad decisions and faced many trials, but God has always been there.

For 25 years, I was in a desert. My phone, electricity, and water were cut off multiple times. I went through years of stress, feeling like I was at my end. I had a stationary bike, and I'd ride and pray, saying, *God, if you could just let me know you're still there.* One day, driving home, I saw the most brilliant rainbow appear as I crested an overpass. It vanished as quickly as it came, but I knew in that moment that it was God's sign that He was there and everything would be okay. He's done that for me countless times.

I owe Him so much. He's always ready to forgive and welcome us back into His arms. I feel so blessed that I need to step up my game and give back to God. I may be 76, but I still have a lot of living to do and a lot to say to you.

SALLY RUSH

My name's Reese Mitchell, and my wife Joy and I have been married for 43 years. We have two grown daughters, two son-in-laws, and a three-

and-a-half-year-old granddaughter. We've been at Church Project for nine years. In September 2020, I was diagnosed with stage four mantle cell lymphoma, a very aggressive form of non-Hodgkin's lymphoma. I had masses behind my eyes, in my neck, lymph nodes, and tonsils. In three weeks, my eyes swelled so badly that one was completely shut.

I asked my oncologist how long I had to live, and he said about three months. I was reluctant to start chemotherapy, scared, and not fully trusting in Jesus. But I knew my family wanted me to try, especially with our granddaughter being so young. On October 4th, 2020, I started my first treatment. By the end of the session, both eyes were open, and after three days, they were completely open. I had no issues with the chemotherapy and handled it very well.

Today, I am still in remission, receiving immunosuppressant treatments every two months and CT scans every six months. Although mantle cell lymphoma is not considered curable, the goal is to maintain remission for as long as possible. My cancer experience humbled me and helped me strip away vanities. I'm not a brave soul, but I want people to know that, without God, it's hard to do anything. No matter our circumstances, God knows them and uses them for His glory. And we should be happy about that. Amen.

REESE MITCHELL

Matthew had a difficult childhood marked by pride, selfishness, and destructive behavior. His life came to a halt one night when he crashed his car at high speed and bled to death. Doctors resuscitated him, but he faced multiple surgeries and a severe brain injury — a long road to recovery. Confused and alone, Matthew searched for a new direction, this time guided by God.

Laying in the hospital bed for 40 days, going mad from the stillness, God used that time as a reset, helping me start from zero. When I first went to counseling, I remember it clearly — it was a God thing. The counselor said, *You were paid for with a high price because God gave His only son for you, and you need to start living like that.* Later, my sister told me, *You're going to a men's conference this weekend.* I thought, *Have you seen me?* But at that conference, I realized I had asked everyone for forgiveness — my sisters, my family — but hadn't asked God to forgive me. I went before Him, saying,

Forgive me for destroying this temple you wanted to build for the Holy Spirit to dwell in. I simply said, *Whatever you want, Lord.* If you want to see God move, tell Him you'll do whatever He wants. The people at CP have such a unique vision — to love Jesus, love each other, and love the world. And through all these challenges, if I could sum it up in one sentence, it's that Jesus won't quit on you.

MATTHEW SHAW

I've always been a foodie and loved baking. Bread has deep meaning, and there's something in the soul that craves its nourishment. I grew up in Utah, wanting to be the best Mormon I could be, striving to be a good girl. My husband and I had many conversations about his addiction, which was sexual in nature and increasingly destructive. Eventually, he was arrested, found guilty, and sentenced to 40 years. I filed for divorce and asked him to leave.

One day, everything I trusted — my marriage, my church, my friends — had failed me. I felt desperate. I was canning peaches, listening to the Narnia movie, when a song, *Wunderkind,* played. I felt God speak to me: *I have a purpose for you, and it has nothing to do with those things. It has everything to do with Me.* Looking up at the stars, I realized that nothing on earth had to do with the man I knew or anyone else — it was all about God.

That night, I felt God say, *I'll take your life and make it beautiful. We've got things to do, and you can be really excited.* He asked for all of me, and I gave it to Him. I didn't know then that I was being saved, but I knew He could do something better with my life.

I began reading the Bible and learning about surrendering to Christ, which was different from what I had been taught. God helped me start my bakery and guided me through the pain of divorce. He lifted me above the wreckage, and even my children felt encouraged and excited. It was God.

CHRISTIN SHUMWAY

Growing up, I went to church with my family every week, but it felt like tradition. I saw God as distant and authoritative, believing I had to earn His approval by following commandments and rituals. As I got older, life became more complicated with broken relationships and failures. I realized it was impossible to earn God's approval on my own, so I ignored the distance between God and me.

When I first heard the Gospel, I wept, realizing what Jesus did on the cross and my own brokenness. I cried out to Him, but my life didn't immediately change. Instead, it sank deeper into hopelessness and sin. I hurt the people I loved, and despite my desire to do what was right, I couldn't. Nothing satisfied me. A series of bad choices led to shame and pain.

Then, newly married, I was invited to church again. I heard the gospel message and wondered if I was truly saved, as I had prayed a prayer years ago. The turning point came when I knew I couldn't continue on the same path. I had to confess, repent, and fully commit my life to Jesus. I joined a small group, began reading Scripture, and fell in love with Him. Little by little, He began transforming me and healing the broken areas of my life.

I realized I didn't have to strive for God's love or approval. Jesus stepped into my brokenness and paid the price for me. He redeemed my shame, my guilt, my marriage, and my children. When I fail, His grace is sufficient, and He forgives me. His burden is light. His love has softened my heart and now life is about sharing His redemptive love with others. It's about Jesus.

SANDRA EATON

How to have Conversations Toward Salvation:
GOODGODGOSPEL.COM

SIX

Discipleship

Everyone can be a disciple maker. Discipleship is people leading people as they follow Christ. Our purpose in life, as followers of Jesus, is to be His disciples. A disciple is someone who loves, follows, and joins Jesus on His mission. Church Project is committed to providing resources and relationships to support and strengthen your spiritual growth.

We define a disciple as someone who is actively engaged in a process of knowing Jesus more deeply and personally. A disciple is growing into an obedient follower by saturating their life with the ways of Jesus and developing a lifestyle of walking with Him. A disciple is serving God and others through their church and continuing to make disciples and produce disciple-makers.

Discipleship is the responsibility of every believer. It means learning to love and serve God at a whole new level. However, we can't experience discipleship alone. Wherever you are in your journey, we will come alongside you. From the initial decision to believe and receive Jesus as your Savior to becoming someone who can effectively disciple another, men, women and students every week are meeting together to follow Jesus more.

Through House Church, more and more adults and students within Church Project are being discipled and discipling others – meeting with one another over simple conversations covering what Scripture says about salvation, reading Scripture, praying, serving, and generosity. Actively, we're making disciples who make disciples by reading Scripture, praying together, and living out the ways of Jesus. And we're making more and more disciples next year.

And we anticipate every adult and student in discipleship continuing to have Good.God.Gospel. conversations throughout our city – taking the gospel into every neighborhood, office building, school, and restaurant – turning secular spaces into sacred spaces.

These are stories of how God has used 1:1 relationships to transform people from new faith, or stunted faith, into disciple makers.

I spent 25 years crisscrossing the country, teaching the Bible and sharing the gospel with hundreds of thousands of people. As a traveling Bible teacher, I spoke in every kind of setting — mega churches, small churches, student camps, leadership conferences, college campuses, school gymnasiums, locker rooms, classrooms, parking lots, and even atop flatbed trucks. I preached from makeshift stages in alleyways, taught in tabernacles and tents, and spoke for major Fortune 500 companies and at the White House. Along the way, I wrote and published 32 books. I loved every minute of it. Over those decades, I was seen and read by many, but the one thing no one could really know about me was that I was a man without a community. I had been seen and heard by many, but I hadn't been known by any.

Jason Shepperd and I have been friends for over 30 years. During my years on the road, Jason launched Church Project. Through a series of providential circumstances, we reconnected, and I shared with him how, despite faithfully serving the church, I had never been rooted in a local body of believers. His response was direct and heartfelt: *Dave, you need this Church! And Church Project needs your skills and vast ministry experience.* That was 11 years ago, and I've served as the Pastor of Discipleship at CP ever since.

Our incredible CP community has impacted me in three very strategic ways.

Righteous Agenda: I returned to the heart of God. I found a church in love with Jesus and learned that the solution to a divided world is the church — a simple, biblical, and relevant church like CP. I always knew that a fully functioning church equals Christ Jesus in the world, but at CP, I saw it in action. Salvation is more than theology — it's life change, up close and personal, brought about by a commitment to Jesus. The evidence of lives changed by contact with Christ is so abundant here at CP that the story can never be fully told. Every year, we continue to make more disciples, helping others love Jesus, live in community, and lead others to do the same.

Redemptive Approach: I found the power of House Church. Doing life week after week with others who had experienced God's grace and knew the redeeming power of Jesus inspired, influenced, and instructed me. Through sustained connection with God's people, I gained insight into what God was doing in my life. Redemption happens when the old, dead areas give way to the presence of Jesus. The word of God applied to the crevices of my soul slowly opened me up again. God healed my heart through our community and showed me a new way to live in Christ.

Relational Authenticity: As a traveling nomad with a demanding ministry schedule, I was hard to pin down. While I had a few long-term friends, even they were at a distance. I had been single my whole life, living and traveling, and knew that when I became part of CP, building relationships would be a priority. At CP, I found people who cared deeply about me, and through those relationships, I met a woman who would become my best friend and, later, my wife. Thank you, Church Project!

DAVE EDWARDS, PASTOR OF DISCIPLESHIP

George and I were high school sweethearts, married less than a year after graduation. We had a tumultuous marriage. I prayed for 30 years for George's salvation. In the last three years, he was diagnosed with cancer. When he asked, *Do I want to die from the blood clot in my heart or the cancer?* it forced us to confront deeper questions: Where are you going? Who will you run to when the time comes?

That's when we began having gospel conversations. George reiterated the gospel to me, and in his last three years, he was a changed man. He wanted to visit his hometown, say goodbye to his parents, and drive three days there and back. During those six days, God healed old hurts and brokenness in our relationship. One evening, while driving home with the sunset in the background, I knew this was the beginning of the end. George passed away two months later.

Becoming a widow shifted everything. I cried out to God, asking, *Who's going to take care of me? What am I going to do now?* In His mercy, God answered, *I will take care of you.* But the second question lingered.

In the ten years since George's death, I transitioned from being a Christian to being a true follower of Christ. One major change was coming to Church Project, although I was initially arrogant about it. I didn't like the lighting or the setup. I even called my daughter-in-law, saying, *There's a great church. I think it'll be wonderful for you.*

She asked, *Who took off Lazarus's death shroud?* I realized I didn't know the answer. I'd read it a thousand times, but I never understood. She explained, *Jesus didn't take it off. He turned to the community.* That's when I started attending House Church regularly. Since then, I've seen God do miraculous things in my life, my family, my House Church, and even strangers. He's truly amazing.

TERESA CARSON, DISCIPLE MAKER

My name's Hunter. I've always been the type to learn the hard way — I needed to burn my hand to know the pot was hot. I did well enough in school to graduate, then got the highest-paying job I could find. I chased promotions and traveled a lot, but even though I was moderately successful and making good money, I wasn't happy. I eventually fell to my knees, saying, *God, I can't do this. What I'm trying to force isn't working. I don't know what I should be doing, but I can't do this anymore.*

Soon after, I met my wife, and we visited several churches before coming to Church Project. I was impressed and thought, *This feels right.* We came back the next week, and it was clear this was where we needed to be. We got involved in our House Church, volunteered at Night to Shine and Back to School Better. Dave Edwards invited my wife to a discipleship lunch, and I assumed I'd be her plus one. I wasn't sure if now was the right time, but I told God, *If you call me, I'll be there.*

The next day, I got a call from Dave inviting me into the discipleship program. Little did I know how much I would grow. Through that process, I gained clarity. Looking back, I saw that the Holy Spirit had been working in my life all along, guiding me to this moment. As flawed as I am, I'm just a guy who showed up, brought my best, and my Bible. There's someone out there who needs to hear what Jesus has to say.

HUNTER FILBIN, DISCIPLE MAKER

I grew up going to church every Sunday — morning, night, and Wednesday. My dad was a preacher, and they taught me to love God and the scriptures, but I didn't truly know God or how to get there. My lifelong battle with anxiety also got in the way.

In 2020, our family hit rock bottom when my daughter went through trauma. Looking back, it could have been worse, but it was a dark time. I found myself praying to God in a way I never had before, and that's when I picked up the Psalms. I began memorizing a prayer from Colossians, the one Paul prays for the Colossians, because I wanted to pray it over my daughter.

I've never practiced it perfectly, but I can say it: *From the day we heard, we have not ceased to pray for you, asking that you be filled with the knowledge of His will in all spiritual wisdom and understanding, so as to walk in a manner worthy of the Lord, fully pleasing to Him, bearing fruit in every good work and increasing in the knowledge of God, being strengthened with all power.*

I could never go back to not knowing His words. I don't know how I survived without them. I never thought I could memorize a single verse, but God allowed me to draw near to Him.

TRACY RUFF, DISCIPLE MAKER

I'm Eric. I grew up in Houston, surrounded by people like Coy, Kevin, and Mark who taught me how to walk with Jesus. I didn't know anything else and thought this was how everyone lived. When we moved here, we quickly got settled into Church Project and joined a House Church. What I love about it is the diversity of stories. People come to Christ at different points in their lives, and we all learn from each other — from those like me who can't remember a time without Jesus, to those recently baptized with a fresh passion for Christ.

At CP, I realized that while someone can walk in on a Sunday, worship, hear teaching, and still not be known, true connection happens in House Church. There's a depth that only comes through intimacy and vulnerability, but even deeper than that, there are one-on-one relationships where true growth happens. Meeting with Tyler, a younger believer about my age,

I realized that having wisdom poured into me for 30 years isn't the norm. It's my responsibility to pour that out and help others. There are things I take for granted that others haven't learned yet, and it's humbling to see how much they benefit.

At its best, it's never one-way—everyone benefits. In any relationship, the depth is determined by what you have in common. And when you open the Word of God with others, your life changes.

ERIC NEWMAN, DISCIPLE MAKER

She had this newfound excitement in her faith. I would sit in the pew on Sundays, sing songs, hear a sermon, but I didn't want to put myself out there. I internalized where I needed God but kept myself at the center, and it didn't feel right. A year later, she signed me up for the Exodus Bible study at Church Project. I resisted, thinking I'd read Exodus enough, but she had already paid the $20, so I went. There, I met Bobby Robbins, who invited me for coffee and told me about a discipleship class. I said, *I'm in.*

Through this class, I realized God had brought her into my life to shatter my hardened heart, put me back on track, and surround me with people to disciple. Now, I disciple five people. Watching broken hearts and struggling marriages be healed, I've seen God work in their lives, and through that, I've had to reflect and change myself. It's strengthened my relationship with my daughter and kept the foundation strong in my marriage.

What stands out most is God's faithfulness to pursue me.

DAN BELCHER, DISCIPLE MAKER

I work for a small sensor company and also help SpaceX build and test rockets. I've always been curious about how God influences things, but never found answers. I was known as *Angry Andy* because of my questions and lack of clarity. Then I met Dan and Clinton at a sports bar trivia night. They were doing Bible study, and after listening to me, Dan invited me to church. I hadn't been in years, but I decided to give it a try. The church was simple: they just read the Bible and discussed it, and later met in House Churches for deeper conversation and prayer.

At first, I thought I didn't belong, but I kept coming back. The more I listened, the more personal the messages became. A sermon on why God allows evil spoke directly to me, and the next one on forgiveness hit even harder, as I struggled with family issues. Then, Dave Edwards preached on Philemon, about being accepted back as a brother without question. It felt like everything was speaking to me directly.

Over time, I realized these weren't coincidences but patterns — God was trying to get my attention. A few months later, on my birthday, Clinton and I were baptized by Dan, with the House Church witnessing it. I reached out to Dave to be there, marking a full circle in my journey. No matter where you are, don't be afraid to talk to others. If they're open to it, the Word will apply to their lives.

ANDY PYNCKEL, DISCIPLE MAKER

I grew up in Conroe, Texas, with my mom, dad, and sister. My dad was always working, and I never had him in my life. By 18, I ended up in prison. The reality of the prison doors shutting hit me hard, and I realized I'd not only ruined my life but also hurt a lot of people, including my one-year-old son and his mother. While in prison, I heard the gospel for the first time. I was told that if I trusted in God, He would pardon me. I feared being judged as a sinner when I met God, and I prayed for His mercy.

One day, while sitting in my bunk, the realization hit me: I had to do things God's way. I renounced my gang ties and gave myself fully to God. I applied to a Christian unit in Texas, where I was quickly accepted — two weeks after applying, when many had been waiting for years. There, I soaked up the teachings and met my Pastor.

When I got out, I still needed guidance. Having grown up without a father, I lacked certain teachings and mentorship. My Pastor became that father figure, investing in my life for the last 12 years. It's not about a course or a book; it's about life-on-life discipleship. He sacrificed and poured into me, and now, I seek to do the same for others, especially in prisons. I give my time, talents, and money, even though I'm not wealthy. I'm passionate about going back to prisons to help those in the same place I was. Just because things don't look the way you expect, doesn't mean God isn't working.

ALEX GARCIA, DISCIPLE MAKER

I came to faith in Jesus as a sophomore in college. Shortly after, I began meeting with a staff member from Cru (formerly Campus Crusade for Christ). We met weekly until I graduated, establishing a solid foundation for my spiritual growth. We studied how to grow spiritually, share my faith, and replicate these truths in others' lives. Since then, I've had the privilege of helping others become disciples who make disciples.

I started attending CP two years ago and was thrilled to find a strong discipleship ministry where disciples are making disciples. It's a joy to work within this ministry, meeting with men to help them grow spiritually, with the goal of equipping them to help others grow as well.

BILL HINSON, CP VAN ALSTYNE

The day I stepped into Church Project in August 2013, I knew it was my church home. I was single at the time and dove into serving, as CP encouraged me to use my time for the Lord. A major part of that time was spent working in Discipleship, where I made many connections and lifelong friendships. After meeting my husband, he joined me at CP, and now my stepson, his mom, and his half-brother also attend regularly. Church Project is a place where sinners are welcome and turned toward Jesus.

EMILY PROSKE, DISCIPLE MAKER

My husband and I have been part of Church Project for over 13 years, and it's been a joy to be part of this body of Christ. The Lord has grown me in many ways and given me opportunities to serve, particularly in One-on-One Discipleship. It's been a privilege to disciple many women, pointing them to Jesus. Some relationships were short, but most were long-term. Many of the women I've discipled are now mature in their faith, serving the Lord in various ways. This, I believe, is what the body of Christ is meant to do — encourage each other in the faith. I see more men and women connecting and discipling others, and it's become part of who we are at CP.

We've also been involved in House Church for all these years — attending, hosting, and my husband serving as an House Church Pastor. As Jason says, this is where we can be real and care for each other. In recent years, we've been recipients of much prayer and support when we needed it. We love our House Church family! I've also been part of our ladies' Bible studies, and between Jason's sermons and our Bible study, I've grown in my ability to study God's word.

It's been a privilege to serve in many ministries and events over the years, like cleaning yards for Angel Reach. CP has always provided ways for us to serve as the hands and feet of Jesus. I'm so thankful for Church Project, the leadership, the staff, and the whole body as we continue to be His lights.

STACEY SCHIERLOH, DISCIPLE MAKER

Growing up in the church, it wasn't my choice—it was my parents' belief. I accepted Christ at 10, prayed with my mom, but the next day, I felt the same. As I got more involved in student ministry, my faith grew deeper each year. The first conversation about God with a friend is always hard. One day, a teammate, who had been trying to regain his faith, and I started talking about God. That conversation led to more, and eventually, I asked if he wanted to be discipled. He thanked me for helping him resolidify his faith. There were times before when I knew God was urging me to speak, but I didn't. I can't rewrite the past, but now, when God tells me to talk to someone, I do it. Talking to people about God is what He calls us to do. He calls us to make disciples, and I truly believe revival is happening right now. It's awesome.

PORTER JOHNSON

I didn't go to church growing up — my grandfather prayed only at Christmas and Thanksgiving. At 19, I met a guy, and we became good friends, working on race cars and talking about the Bible. For a couple of years, that's what we did until life led me in another direction. After getting married, having a son, and then separating, I met Tracy about two years after my divorce. She was a miracle of God. One day, we had lunch with some of her friends, and they spoke about their church and Pastor. I had questions about Jesus being both God's son and God, so we talked for two hours. I told Tracy we needed to find the church and visit the next Sunday. When we pulled into the parking lot, I stopped and said, *We can't be at church.* She asked why, and I realized, *We used to buy beer here, and guys are wearing hats and shorts.* But then I saw everyone with Bibles, and I didn't have mine. The connection in House Church was unlike anything I'd ever experienced. On the second night, I asked Dan if he would do discipleship with me, and he lit up, saying, *I'd love to, brother.* That was three and a half years ago, and we still meet every Monday. Through that, we met Andy at trivia night. He came over, asked if we had beer and Bibles, and said, *I have questions.* After three weeks of talking with him, I experienced my first real spiritual joy. That was God working, not me. I was just there with a Bible.

CLINTON HOWETH, HOUSE CHURCH PASTOR

Many things make Church Project great: the teaching, House Churches, simplicity for generosity, and the company of others drawn to these values. But it is discipleship at CP that has had the greatest impact on my walk with Christ. During the early days of Covid, Dave Edwards cold-called people about discipleship. When he contacted me, I felt an undeniable call to get involved. I had informally discipled others but never as part of a church outreach.

When I met with Dave and others, I was struck by the simple yet profound process for one-on-one discipleship, leading to deep conversations, Bible study, and lasting change. Since then, I've discipled many men, watched them grow in the Lord, and seen the Spirit radically transform our walks with Jesus. As Paul told Timothy, *For God has not given us a spirit of timidity, but of power and love and discipline.* I am so grateful Church Project takes Jesus' command to make disciples seriously. Nothing compares to the impact of meeting one-on-one with others to pursue a deeper relationship with the Lord.

GARRETT DICKSON, DISCIPLE MAKER

SEVEN

Global Missions

Everyone can go somewhere. Church Project's global mission has always been rooted in partnership, and over the years, we have seen God work through these connections. We send short-term teams around the world to serve alongside local churches and ministries, working hand-in-hand with pastors and leaders to meet needs and share the love of Jesus. These trips have been as much about learning, encouraging, and being transformed by the people we meet as they have been about giving. Through these experiences, we've witnessed God build lasting relationships and strengthen the global church.

By God's grace, our global outreach has grown, and we are committed to continue with a broader vision. Church Project doesn't just send teams; we also support missionaries both spiritually and financially. In doing so, we help strengthen the local church and bring the gospel to places where it has yet to be heard. We've seen God use our people to bring hope to areas of deep need.

Looking ahead, we expect more men, women, and families answering the call to spread the gospel to unreached people groups around the world, to have powerful Good.God.Gospel. conversations and to lead the way in establishing more House Churches, which will then multiply into new Church Projects, expanding the reach of the gospel even further.

We also look forward to increasing the number of global trips, offering more opportunities for everyone to go somewhere each year.

God has used Church Project to change the way people see Christ, Christians, and the Church, not just here in The Woodlands or in the United States, but around the world.

These are stories of how God has used Church Project to affect other contexts and cultures in sharing the gospel and planting more churches.

An unreached people group is a particular identifiable group. Usually they have language and common history, customs and culture, and live within a determined boundary. So a misconception of an unreached people group is that someone deep in the heart of an African tribe, or somewhere buried in the Amazon, unreached people groups can be very well educated, living in major cities.

For instance, the unreached people group, one of them this week for prayer is North Africans living in Canada with only like one-tenth of a percent of them who know Jesus. I am considered a storyteller or an Arabic. It's I would be called a hacker. Whatever. And so I learn. God's encounters with his people and with those that he loves.

I learned those scriptures by heart. I call them power encounters, where God intervenes in a human life and reveals who he is by what he does, rather than what he says.

I have a shopping list of ways I would love to see my church engaged. And one of them is to be praying. To be praying for unengaged people groups and unreached people groups, to actually know them by name and to commit to praying for them. I believe that the going has to start with prayer. And so I think the natural outcome of intense prayer for the rest of the world would be the fact that then God would ask people of Church Project to go, that they would feel the call like Isaiah did when he says, who will go? Who will we send? And that actually my vision is that 75 individuals from Church Project will say, here I am. Send me.

I believe part of it is education, that people would begin to understand that there are still millions of people who have never heard anything about eternity, and how it can be theirs through believing in the Lord Jesus Christ, the gospel. So I believe that education is one that we begin to speak regularly about the unreached and the unengaged in the world.

And I believe, as we do, that with our children, and we do that with our teams, and we do that amongst ourselves in our house, churches, and even from the podium on Sunday, constantly remembering those that have not heard. I believe that's the first step, because I believe then God will lean on our hearts to want to be a part of what he's doing and to pray God's heart.

This is God's heart is for people to know who he is. He has never changed. He is still busy at work.

THE STORYTELLER, MISSIONARY IN THE MIDDLE EAST

In 1993, my family immigrated here, but I never truly connected with their story until I started serving my neighbors. I was called to deny myself, carry my cross, and follow Christ. If He did it for me, why can't I do it for others? I was expecting to see lines of people, but what humbled me was the work we did, like cleaning up trash, rat tomatoes, and crates. Every task had purpose. The Lord says, *Whatever you do for others, you do for me,* and that has been a challenge, but also very special.

Every Thursday, we share the gospel with over 400 people. It's not about us; we simply ask the Lord to make it happen. Though we may not see the immediate impact, the difference we make is monumental. Hearing story after story about people who needed help and received it at the right time is incredible. I didn't realize how often the Bible talks about helping the foreigner, the one out of their land. We're all foreigners; we all need saving. It's humbling because, often, we get judgmental and focus on outward beauty, but true beauty is eternal and spiritual, seen through the hand of God.

JENN MOYA, SOUTH TEXAS TRIP

In 2011, after taking a class called The Quest for Authentic Manhood, I had a desire to serve others, especially in Africa. My first mission trip to Kenya was life-changing, not because of the safari, but because of the people. While driving near the Indian Ocean, I saw people digging in a dry riverbed for water, using orange juice containers to fill jerrycans. It was unbelievable. When I returned to Houston, I immediately wanted to go back.

I had another chance to visit Kenya, then went to Malawi. While sharing a Bible story with villagers, I felt God urging me to ask if they wanted to receive Christ. That day, 40 people accepted or rededicated their lives to Christ. It was one of the top five most impactful moments of my life.

On a flight from Nairobi to London, I met a man who had climbed Mount Kilimanjaro for a fundraiser. The idea sparked in me, and I decided to climb it for my 60th birthday. But as I studied Isaiah, God convicted me that my plans were selfish. I realized it wasn't about me. So, I moved the climb off my birthday and made it a fundraiser for Child Legacy. Since then, I've led 11 teams, raised $2.5 million, and impacted 4.5 million people.

God orchestrated everything, one step at a time, leading me to this mission. I now see my life as a series of steps, each one preparing me for what He's called me to do.

MIKE NAVOLIO, CLEAN WATER CLIMB

I'd invite anyone to join the believers at Church Project to pray for unreached people groups and the persecuted church. A decision to follow Christ often moves individuals from one list to another. Will they be kicked out, arrested, forced into unwanted marriages, lose their children, risk trafficking, or be denied opportunities? I pray they find healthy church homes with shepherds who can care for them and possibly refuge in cities like Houston, where Church Project partners with organizations like Houston Welcomes Refugees. May we each take up the mantle of Galatians 6:10: "Therefore, as we have opportunity, let us do good to all, especially to those who are of the household of faith."

GAIL BIELITZ

I never believed in myself or my worth. I grew up in poverty, in a family of six, living in a mud house, often going days without food. Sometimes we ate rotten food from trash cans. I was bitter and didn't believe God existed.

When I joined Compassion, I thought it was about food, but I learned it was about love and care. I received acceptance, learned to pray, and read the Bible. My sponsors taught me that poverty doesn't determine your future— it shapes it.

Now, as I help others, I'm grateful for my story because I understand their struggles. When they talk about hunger or grief, I've experienced it.

I lost both my parents, and I know the pain of loss. When I moved into Rehema House, God provided for my mom's surgery, but she passed away. Later, my dad passed as well. Each time something good happened, I faced another loss.

But through it all, God remains faithful. Even when I want to quit, I remember I have a purpose and that His grace is enough. Working at Rehema House is hard, but it's fulfilling. I've rescued girls who were abandoned, offering them hope and telling them of God's greatness. If they see Jesus through me, then it's worth everything. This is not my story—it's God's story.

MAUREEN, MERCY HOUSE GLOBAL

Over the past year, God has been growing me in many ways, teaching me that He is a global God, and I am part of His global church and mission. When the opportunity arose in March to join a mission trip to the South Texas border with Church Project, I knew I couldn't miss it.

Before the trip, I didn't fully understand the humanitarian crisis at the border or what to expect. This trip, however, was unlike any other mission experience I had. We partnered with the local church, witnessing how God is using His people to care for the foreigner and sojourner in a desperate place. The local church's faithfulness and God's movement in the area were encouraging.

Serving asylum seekers, we heard the stories of families who risked everything to flee their countries. We were moved by one family's testimony of God making His name known as they crossed the border. It became clear that the border issue is complex, and oversimplifying or speaking out without understanding can cause harm.

God used every person I met to change my perspective on the border. He captured my heart for the foreigner and sojourner. While immigration is a polarizing issue, as Christians, our response matters. We serve a God who loves the foreigner, and we are called to do the same.

MACKENZIE ELLIOTT, SOUTH TEXAS TRIP

I didn't know if missions were still in my future, but through little yeses and trusting God, I found myself in Nigeria. When I first landed, my luggage didn't arrive, and doubts began to creep in. I was alone, homesick, and unsure if I was truly trusting God or just following an open door. In that room, the only thing I had was my Bible, and it became a tool for surrender.

Being in a place where Christians are persecuted, with no control over my situation, redefined trust for me. I thought I had already surrendered, but this experience deepened that surrender.

During soccer camps in different towns, I heard about a church that had been burned and soccer goals stolen by Muslims. Despite this, the people had more joy than I had ever seen, a joy we don't see in the United States. On the last day of camp, families from both Christian and Muslim backgrounds gathered, and I witnessed the miracle of unity — smiling faces, joy shared by everyone.

On my first Sunday back, I felt bittersweet. While it was sweet to be home, I couldn't shake the feeling that my life had changed. God is so much bigger than I could have imagined.

LEILA ANDERSON, SHORT-TERM MISSIONARY IN NIGERIA

I'm involved in House Church and Women's Bible study, but I wanted to step out of my comfort zone and see God working around the world. After talking to a lady in my House Church who encouraged me to go on a mission trip, I brought it to my husband, expecting him to shut it down, but he was incredibly supportive. Nervous about what to expect, I was reassured by my roommate, an ex-Marine, and another team member who had been on 30 mission trips.

One of the most memorable moments was giving glasses to people who truly needed them. I'll never forget a three-year-old boy who had poor eyesight; when he put on the glasses, he started running around in excitement.

I didn't realize how close you become serving alongside others, or how welcoming the people in Guatemala were. On our last day, we visited villages with the VBS and water filter teams, and it was eye-opening to see their living conditions. Despite having so little, they were so generous, offering us chairs and letting us hold their children.

It taught me that hospitality isn't about material things but about the heart's openness to others. We all have spiritual, emotional, or relational needs, and through the love of Jesus, we can help meet those needs. The connection we made, even without speaking the same language, was powerful, especially when we prayed together. It was a moment I'll never forget.

JENNY ADAMS, GUATEMALA TRIP

We often say Malawi is a God-fearing nation, but when I visit the communities, I see a different reality. People are deeply rooted in traditional beliefs and aimlessly searching for something tangible that offers hope. Hope is the force that drives people to move forward — whether as individuals, communities, or a nation.

The land where we work with Child Legacy used to be considered a cursed place, but now it's a fertile miracle. We've brought a message of hope for the future, transforming the community over the past few decades. Without Child Legacy, I can't imagine what this place would look like.

Through our platform, we teach the word of God and preach Jesus. I've seen mothers come to Christ, even on their sickbeds. Some have asked me to pray before surgery, and in those moments, I share the gospel. It's humbling to see them receive Christ in such vulnerable moments.

Economic growth, social development, and the gospel of Jesus Christ are key. Whenever we repair a well, we also share the gospel. We have two Pastors on staff who lead Bible training twice a week, ministering to people in the wards. Spreading God's word gives them hope—not in man, but in God. That's the true hope that drives people forward.

YOHANN CHIKWATU, CP MALAWI

I went to church every week, prayed daily, but was lost for the first 28 years of my life. This experience fuels my passion for sharing the gospel. Since I was 15, I knew I was double-minded. It wasn't until I had my first two children and dedicated them that I realized I didn't want them to be the same, but I had no idea how to lead them differently.

In preparation for a mission trip, I felt led to study 1st and 2nd Peter, meditating on the verse: "We may declare the praises of him who called us out of darkness into his glorious light." I was asked to lead the discipleship portion of the soccer clinic, which excited me, though the children we were serving were older than expected. Nervous, I prayed, asking God to help me speak His word and forget myself. God was faithful.

During the clinic, I noticed two girls sitting by themselves. One had just been diagnosed with a serious disease, and her fear of death was overwhelming. I listened, hugged, prayed, and shared Jesus with her. Over time, she opened up more, and we cried and prayed together.

Reflecting on how many people heard the gospel, I feel humbled and privileged to be part of it. Jesus revealed Himself powerfully throughout the trip. When we do His work, He is always with us, working through us.

INGRID BENDER, GUATEMALA TRIP

Adjusting to life in a new country has been a lot — good, but hard. It's like relearning everything you thought you knew, from turning on the oven to buying groceries. It's been a challenging transition, but also beautiful seeing God's kindness and learning to depend on Him in ways we never have before.

Getting sick right after we arrived was tough, and parenting in a busy apartment was a challenge. But one thing that stood out was the presence of refugees and people begging. One man asked me to buy trash bags, but I offered to buy him lunch instead, and we spent time hearing about his difficult life. He was interested in joining a Bible study at our church, which was an amazing outcome.

Please pray for our language learning, especially for Easton as he's started full-time school, and for building good local friendships. I also want to thank God for the support we've received from Church Project, for the opportunity to serve this community full-time, and for how well our kids have adapted to the transition. Shelby volunteers at a center for single moms and kids, and I'm involved in a financial class for people in desperate need. We're part of a small church with strong believers wanting to make a big impact in an unreached area, and we are grateful for all of it.

ZACH & SHELBEY BILLINGTON, MISSIONARIES IN ECUADOR

Alaska is a beautiful place with a lot of brokenness. You know, I always knew there was a need up here, but, you didn't really know how real it was to get here. And you're here for ten minutes. We were here for the first night, and they gave us case files for these kids. And it shows what they've been through. I had two campers at first that I was going to be with and their brothers. And, I mean, when I open that case file and see that their mom was a heroin addict and their father beat them with his belt every night. And then when they were taken into custody, they're covered in bruises and have scars. I mean, you think who deserves that? God did a lot of special things here. And, you know, it's really special when you can see it happening. And I think that being able to apply that, that idea of loving on another person that you don't even know. I think that if we just all did that, that we can just make the world such a better place and we could help heal some of this brokenness that's come on, others. And it's crazy what just being someone's friend can do.

AUSTIN MORGAN, ALASKA TRIP

This October marked my 4th South Texas Mission Trip, and the primary impact of these trips has been learning through scripture about God's heart for the foreigner, remembering that we are all foreigners on this earth. Over these four trips, I've developed deep friendships with our guides at Border Perspectives, local ministry partners, and fellow travelers from Church Project. There are two trips a year, one in the spring and one in the fall.

My motivation to go is to leave the comfort of The Woodlands and spend 4 days in the beauty and brokenness of South Texas. South Texas is rich in both its people and Mexican culture, but the brokenness is seen in the wall separating the U.S. from Mexico and Central America.

Each trip is similar but unique. We leave CP early Sunday morning in 8-passenger vans for the 7-hour drive, where you learn a lot about your fellow travelers. The first day is spent visiting local historic sites and meeting with US Customs officers. The second, third, and fourth days are spent working with local ministry partners like Iglesia Misionera Cristo Vive, Catholic Charities Respite Center, Border Mission, and Team Brownsville. We return to The Woodlands early Friday morning.

Each morning begins with a devotional to understand God's heart for the foreigner and how this should shape our posture towards loving them today.

ALEC LIS

Church Project has played a crucial role in my relationship with Jesus. Since coming to know the Lord at 13, I've had a heart to share what God has done in my life. In high school, I learned there are about 3 billion people who have never heard the name of Jesus, and probably never will unless someone goes to tell them. After high school, I went on a 9-month mission trip, growing in my understanding of God's heart for every nation, tribe, and tongue. I saw thriving Biblical communities in Central America and Africa, where House Churches met weekly to study the Word and pray. I returned with a passion to see the unreached reached with the Gospel in my neighborhood and the nations!

One evening, I came across a message from CP with Jason Pierce talking about Acts 2 and unreached people groups. I felt the Lord pressing me to attend a gathering. A few weeks later, I went to the first Wednesday gathering, and the first person I saw was Jason. During the service, they prayed for the Balloqui family as they prepared to serve in the Middle East. Mike Navolio then shared about climbing Mount Kilimanjaro to seek God's direction for his ministry. This left me in awe of what God was doing at Church Project, and I wanted to be a part of it!

The Lord has strategically gifted us with the local church to encourage one another. I've met amazing men and women passionately in love with Jesus. I started working at Good City Coffee and witnessed God at work through gospel conversations with people from all walks of life. I got plugged into a House Church and began attending Prayer for the Nations and young adults gatherings. I'm excited about what God is doing in these days and the role of the local church in bringing His glory to the ends of the earth!

EMILY KNOLLENBERG

After my second deployment to Iraq, God made me realize he kept me safe for a purpose — that my life wasn't my own but was meant to be used for his glory. I had no idea what that would look like until close friends told us they were going to work with unreached people in a village in Asia. I thought it sounded ridiculous. They had sat in the same pews and Bible studies as us, and I couldn't understand why they would do that. They exposed us to new authors, sermons, and ideas, and suddenly it hit me — the

Bible has a missional plan for the world.

This revelation brought excitement to return to the call God had placed on our lives. He opened doors in ways only he could. Each people group is a unique reflection of God's image, and the way they sing, dance, and live is not to be changed but embraced as part of the greater picture of praise to the Lamb in Revelation. Our mission is to love these people and expose them to the Word of God, helping them gather and grow the church with the tools they need.

Family is a blessing, and it reminds us that our children are never truly ours but are gifts from God. We rely on him fully, and that trust makes everything clearer. Our kids need to know that the youth group is praying for them and that the House Church families haven't forgotten them. They'll be loved, embraced, and remembered when they return. We're not just doing ministry to the unreached; we're also showing this church how worthy Jesus is of everything we have, and inviting them into the joy of partnership.

MISSIONARY PARENTS IN EAST ASIA

EIGHT

Generosity

Everyone can be a generous giver. We operate with simplicity for the sake of generosity. And when we give our time and our finances to Church Project, we join together in strengthening this church and in supporting Ministry Partners who meet needs and share the love of Christ.

Church Project has given almost $16.5 million to church planting and ministries, locally and globally, in the last 15 years. By the generosity of many, Church Project has had the ability to greatly impact the future of our Ministry Partners, here and around the world, and support new Church Projects and other churches alike. Together, your giving has met many needs in our city and our world and advanced the gospel to many.

And in the last 15 years, God has done great things through His church From January 10, 2010, with 40 people, in two House Churches and one simple Sunday Gathering in an obscure, rented warehouse, with no phone number, no foyer receptionist and no traditional marketing methods, we now have many dozens of multiplying House Churches in The Woodlands, TX. We have thousands of people gathering weekly in two Sunday Gatherings. We have supported 20+ Church Project church plants. And we have supported, encouraged and resourced many other churches beyond Church Projects. And many Ministry Partners and others have started by people within Church Project.

We operate with a theology of space that says "space is not sacred, but sacred things happen in space." This allows us to use our three buildings for very sacred things. But also, we *share* our space with ministries in our city on a regular basis – hundreds of times a year. And we *steward* our space by renting it out at below market numbers that allow people to have a great space for their events, while also capturing income to pursue our goal of being mortgage neutral. This allows more and more giving to go towards gospel movement and good ministries.

We devote ourselves to being generous. Jesus calls us to be generous. Generosity is a gift of God's grace. The only model of giving we see in Scripture are people giving to the local church – practiced for thousands of years.

Jesus sees what we give. He saw the rich and the poor alike bringing their offerings to the temple as part of worship. He sees our hearts, our faith, what we depend on, what we keep for ourselves, our motives - He sees it all. He notices what we do in all areas, even in the area of our finances and giving.

Giving is an act of worship. In the Old Testament, they brought gifts to the temple. In the New Testament, they brought money and laid it at the apostles' feet. Worship how we declare God's worth in our lives: singing, praying, obedience, knowing Scripture, and giving. Generosity is a big deal to God because it is an act of worship.

Giving is for everyone, all the time. We give in the times when we are rich, when we have plenty, when no needs are unmet, when we have security for the future. We give in the times when we are poor, when we don't have enough, when what we give could be used greatly. Regular giving allows God to work on His timetable, not ours.

Giving is about faith. Jesus didn't need an accountant (although He had one on His staff) to know that the widow gave less money. And yet, He acknowledged she still gave more. Out of greater faith. And that's what is behind our generosity. Jesus was looking for who gave greater faith in their giving.

These are just a few stories of how God has changed our hearts and minds in the way we give generously to His plans and purposes.

Well, I heard about this Jason talk on stage about we're gonna be building a community clinic, it's gonna help the impoverished and the unfortunate in our community. And I said, that's something I can definitely get behind.

I've been blessed and fortunate and I have a lot of resources available to me. I'm a construction superintendent, so I asked Jason, *Hey, can I be part of this?* He says, *Absolutely.* And so I gathered some of those resources. We're helping get this clinic done. Hopefully it'll be done early this upcoming year.

I asked my plumber, I said, *Hey Lewis, we're building a community clinic, is this something that you'd like to be part of?* He says, *Absolutely, count me in.* I'm donating a hundred percent of my labor. Same thing with my electrician, same thing with my framing subcontractor. He's right now, he's not taking my money.

What's the saying? Preach the gospel always. It's just not a place to come and go to church on Sunday. It's not just a place to, uh, to say, *Oh, that's my church,* as you're driving by. It's to show the example. I mean, that's what we're doing. So it makes me feel good helping out.

JERRY COOK

Amy: My parents took us to church. We passed the collection plate around probably every Sunday. Money was never really discussed in my family, so it wasn't an area that I grew up with a lot of knowledge or education about. My parents just always took care of us.

Noel: I had a good example of what it looked like to be faithful in giving and good stewards of money. Unfortunately, I didn't take that great example into college. That's when I started to accumulate my own debt and manage that pile of as much as I could before I got married. So I got to bring that to my wife.

Amy: I had a lot of resentment towards Noel, feeling like she had lived selfishly, that his past choices were being brought into our relationship.

Noel: It didn't take long into the process to see it working. As long as you're committed to it, it's going to work.

Amy: I was in my late 20s. Noel's in his early 30s. All of our friends were going out. They were at restaurants. They were taking trips. They looked super cool. And they're cool clothes. And Noel and I had a teeny tiny budget, like $20 a week to do fun stuff because we were committed to getting our feet underneath us financially. When we were so focused on getting out of our huge pile of debt, it was really hard to say, okay, we're also going to tithe. We're going to tithe first before we do anything else because God has provided us with this money. It's his. He calls us to give it to him joyfully. And so we did.

Noel: We knew God to be faithful previously. We knew he'd be faithful in the future. And so... right. Do what you're going to do. This is yours. And we're just trusting you're going to make ends meet. And so we gave, and it was great to be a part of a new... we were a part of God's ministry just by giving.

Amy: Some checks started coming in the mail that we were not expecting. We had to call the company and be like, did you mean to send this to us? Should we cash this? The Lord just really provided for us financially in the next season in a way that we were not expecting, and totally surprised us. And what we learned through that is that God honors obedience. We know it won't always be financial, or it might be a wonderful season in my marriage, or it might be blessings to my children. It could be many different forms of God providing for us.

Noel: Money is a tool he has given us, and so he controls that. And we're not ruled by ones and zeros, and how much we've got in an account. It's what he has told us to do, and we're just going to be faithful to that.

NOEL & AMY JOHNSON

I was the youngest of six kids, and the sister next to me, three years older than I, always was born with special needs.

When you have somebody always in need in your house, you tend to forget about yourself and start looking more at how you can help others. Mom would have a saying, she'd say, *When you start feeling sorry for yourself, start thinking of somebody else and how you can help them.*

It's not easy, especially in the teenage years. I think when I got out on my own, I started depending on God more. He became my protector, and I started making that realization like, *Oh, there was a pattern to my life back then.* I would go to church every week and I had friends, and that's what drew me back, thinking, I *need this. I need the structure in my life. I need these people in my life.*

And so I started looking for a church. I found a church and one of the questions was, *How are you serving other people?* I was a labor and delivery nurse at that time, and I realized at that point that was a blessing — it really was—to be in somebody's life because you're in either the most joyful time in a person's life, or it can be the most devastating.

I think it's something you learn as you're growing up, and you start to realize Christmas is not nearly as much fun opening up the presents as seeing the thing that you gave to somebody else.

Well, when you get to give to somebody else, and it means so much towards the kingdom of God and His word being spread, you can do so much.

It's a privilege to be able to hand out God's money. It's not really mine, right? It's a blessing that was given to Jerry and I, and it continues to bless us, and we've always tithed.

It's not just the job of helping, it's also the people that you're meeting while you're there. You see how God's working in their lives and you get to know them. You could go out and do something good for people. You could join other organizations that do good, but that's where it stops. With the church, you're also giving them Jesus, and you're giving them hope for eternity.

NELL SAGEHORN

Jennifer: We grew up as friends and later got married at a young age. I've been tithing since childhood, taught by my mom.

Tim: At first, it felt like just an obligation — something I did because I had to. But attending a crusade in '98 was a turning point for us. That's when we truly understood the gospel and what giving really meant. A year after moving to Texas, the Crowes invited us to start a House Church in our home. That was almost five years ago, and it's been a blessing to see this community grow. We've met people from all backgrounds and life stages, all learning about Christ together. At the end of the day, we're all there for each other. Tithing has always been part of our lives, but giving beyond that is where our faith has grown. We encourage others to try it, not for prosperity, but because God promises blessings when we give.

Jennifer: At Church Project, we know our gifts are going toward something meaningful, and it's a joy to be part of a church that prioritizes generosity and simplicity. You can't sit at Church Project and be idle.

Tim: It all comes down to the fact that Christ made the ultimate sacrifice for us, and in response, how can we not give some small portion back to Him?

TIM & JENNIFER CLOUTHIER, HOUSE CHURCH HOSTS

Craig: So for me, backstory, I grew up in a really small town. I went to a traditional Protestant church with the gold shiny offering plates. And I saw my mom put the check in every week, but I had no idea what it was, how much, or what it was for.

Rae Anne: I was saved at a young age, thankfully, beautifully raised in a home where giving was important.

Craig: Fast forward, I go to college, graduated college, and I started working actually at a church. And the pledge drive came around. I pledged maybe $500 and that was it. For the year? Yeah, for the year. And then out of sight, out of mind, didn't think anything of it. And then around October I got the form letter from the church that said, *Hey, you pledged $500. Um, it's coming near the end, and you've given $0.* So I was like, okay, I messed up. So I paid almost all 500 right then. I was eating a lot of ramen, beans, and rice.

Rae Anne: I struggle with having a generous heart and a generous spirit. Like when it's time to give, I'm doing that internal mind check of having a scarcity complex or counting up the dollars or thinking about what else I could do. It's not something that I'm proud of. It's something that's my flesh. It's what I am struggling with.

Craig: The day you lost your job, we were devastated. We're trying to distract ourselves watching TV, and then the doorbell rang. It was a neighbor from down the street who we knew, and he was like, *Hey, I have some coupons for free dinners.* In that moment, we both thought, *God's going to watch out for us. We're going to be okay.*

Rae Anne: He even gave us our first meal, literally. I was unemployed for 10 months, and it made no sense to keep giving. But I was like, no, the Lord has not released us from this. So we were faithful. At the end of the 10 months, our checking account had a higher balance than when we began, and our savings were never touched. It made no sense, because it was God's sense, and He can do anything.

Craig: I've heard some people say, *Well, if I can't give the 10%, I shouldn't give anything. I can't start giving until I can do that.* Even though my 500 was nowhere near 10%, it was a start.

Rae Anne: And the Holy Spirit planted that. Then He asked me to give half. We very slowly, it was a journey, and we slowly, incrementally increased it from 2.5% more to 5% more. And when I got a raise, we were driving home, and I said, *Honey, I think it's time to give more. And it's going to hurt. But I think it's what we're asked to do.* So we very slowly, it was a journey, and we slowly, incrementally increased it. We live with a God who is a God of abundance.

CRAIG & RAE ANNE DODDS,
HOUSE CHURCH PASTOR & WIFE

Take your next step in generosity. You can start giving a little. If you are a part of Church Project but not yet giving to Church Project, would you begin to give regularly? If 2,000 of us, who are not yet giving, begin to give $20/week, our giving would increase by $1 million annually.

You can start giving a tithe. Maybe you have given some, and your next step could be giving what Scripture considers 10%. This act of obedience could be transformative in leveraging your finances for doing good and increasing your own trust in God.

You can give above and beyond. If you give generously and consistently, you may desire to give more through an additional gift. This gift would realize Church Project's efforts in planting more churches, supporting Ministry Partners, and so much more.

Give to Church Project: CHURCHPROJECT.ORG/GIVE

NINE

Care

Care means a lot for the health of a local church. Jesus is our model for care. And He calls us to love others the same way He loves us. We have House Church as our main pathway for connection and care. We see this in more ways that we can count – in the way House Church Pastors lead weddings and funerals and in how House Churches join together to meet financial, emotional and spiritual needs for one another. We also see this heightened level of care through focused Support Groups.

From counseling partners within our church and locally to actively participating in seasonal Support Groups, we've seen hundreds of men, women and families experience healing, freedom and breakthrough with God. And we're thankful for the men and women who have used their own stories to encourage and equip others through Support Groups like Waiting in Hope, GriefShare, our fostering & adoption community and more.

These are some of the stories of how marriages have been made and mended, how the childless have become parents, how those addicted have been made free, and how the grieving have gained deeper gratitude and joy for God.

In our 12 years connected to Church Project, we've walked through many seasons of life: engagement, newlyweds, Pastoral ministry, figuring out marriage and family in ministry, miscarriages, raising 3 children, fostering... In reflecting on each of these seasons, we're humbled by the fact that we've been known and loved like family by people beyond our biological family, because this church is family.

We've grown up here. We've seen others grow up here. It's a unique perspective that not everyone gets to experience. And through both beautiful and challenging seasons alike, our relationships with the Body of Christ and with Jesus have sweetened and deepened.

House Church has been a cornerstone of our being at Church Project. And as any family does, our House Church family has grown and multiplied and morphed over the years. But through each of these changes, our network of people who care about us and who have walked through life with us has only widened.

These changes are rarely easy. When change happens within a church family, in our culture, it is far more common to jump ship rather than grow through the pain. It feels rare in our world for people to stay in one place when conflict or boredom arises. But since Jesus has planted our family here, he has drawn us closer to him, deepened our trust in his perfect plans, and discipled us by His Word and His people.

How can we sum up our 12 years here? We can't. We can simply say that we're experiencing God in this place (Father, Son, and Holy Spirit). The promises of God are true and good. Jesus is our satisfaction and rest. The Holy Spirit is powerful and sustaining. His Church is beautiful and essential.

CALVIN (PASTOR OF CARE & CONNECTIONS)
& LINDSAY TAYLOR

I've been at Church Project since October 8, 2017, and it has been such a blessing for me and my daughter. When I first started, I was a single mom with Cerebral Palsy. I joined the women's Bible study, went on the Women's Retreat with the CP Single Moms Ministry, joined a House Church, and got baptized on May 27, 2018. It was the best day of my life, aside from having my daughter.

Then, on March 27, 2019, my life changed forever. I became bedridden, unable to leave my apartment, and in chronic pain every day. Church Project, Project Abilities, and my House Church stepped in, loving and helping me and my daughter for almost six years. They've kept my eyes on Jesus through it all. My House Church has provided support, meals, helped us move, been with me in the hospital, taken care of me after surgeries, and celebrated birthdays and holidays with us. They live in the trenches with me, lifting me up when I'm down and celebrating Jesus with me on the good days.

Church Project has also given me purpose through serving in our online gatherings. I'm now dependent on others for everything, and if it weren't for Jesus bringing me to Church Project eight years ago, I wouldn't have made it through my trials. I'm so blessed and beyond thankful for this beautiful community of believers. Happy 15th Anniversary, Church Project! I love you all!

TIFFANY MCCLINTOCK

My wife and I were introduced to CP by our best friends, who invited us to the marriage workshops Hans and Star hosted. We attended the first two, driving from Pasadena, TX, and it was well worth it. In July, we moved to Spring and have been attending since. We truly appreciate the environment, the way the Bible is taught, shared, and lived out among the congregation. From the greeters to the people leaving with love and patience, it feels like home. CP has helped strengthen our marriage, and we appreciate the hospitality that makes everyone feel welcome. We'll continue attending and inviting others for that reason.

OMMAR & GABRIELA CASTILLO

When my family first walked through the doors of Church Project 13 years ago, we were broken with two small children after a long journey of infertility and multiple pregnancy losses. We hadn't been to church in years, despite being raised in the church. Today, both our children are in student ministry, and it's amazing to see how God has healed our hearts and grown us.

I always thought being a Christian meant following rules — going to church, reading the Bible, and praying. But what I've learned at Church Project is about sanctification. I'll never forget hearing Jason say, *You don't want to be the same person you are today, 5, 10, or 15 years from now!* That clicked for me — this walk is about continual growth.

God has used Church Project to teach me, from serving in Project Kids to discipleship, meeting one-on-one with others to examine Scripture and walk closer to the Lord. Through this community, I've grown through both heartache and joy. Leading Waiting in Hope, an infertility and pregnancy loss ministry at CP, has grown me in ways I never imagined. God healed my heart through this ministry and allowed me to help women struggling in the same way, pointing them to Jesus, the only source of hope.

13 years ago, a simple tagline — *Biblical. Simple. Relevant.* — drew us to Church Project, and God has used this church in countless ways to sanctify us and help us serve others.

BRANDY SHELTRAW, WAITING IN HOPE

In 2017, I met my now husband, Nathan, through the Unmarrieds Life Connection Group at CP. I joined the group hoping to find friendships with others in the same life stage. I wasn't looking for a romantic relationship, as I had already told God that if He wanted me to have one, He would have to make it happen organically. And that's exactly what He did.

Fast forward to May 2018 — Nathan and I were married in the foyer of the CP building on Sawdust, with Barry Bathea, Nathan's mentor and discipleship leader, officiating the ceremony.

STACEY BOWDEN

Matthew: Our oldest was four when our youngest, Amelia, was born. Life was chaotic with four little ones, lots of diapers, and just trying to keep our heads above water. At 18 months, we noticed bruising on Amelia, which we chalked up to rough play.

Misty: But at her pediatric appointment, I mentioned her symptoms, and the doctor immediately ordered bloodwork. Before I could even get to the car, the doctor called, urging us to go straight to the ER. Within minutes, we learned that Amelia had leukemia. Matthew and I prayed like never before, and God quickly led us to St. Jude Children's Research Hospital in Memphis.

Matthew: Her treatment was tough, with many ups and downs. We spent a summer together, making memories, not knowing if we'd have months, weeks, or even days left with her. Sadly, ten days later, after a relapse, she passed away.

Misty: The pain was indescribable, and for four years, I struggled with anger and grief. I couldn't grieve in the same way as Matthew, and vice versa. Eventually, I reached a point where I was ready to reconcile my relationship with God. That's when I found a GriefShare group. Unlike other experiences, this group gave me hope and a perspective on grieving that allowed me to see God's light again.

MATTHEW & MISTY TAYLOE, GRIEFSHARE

Kelly: I saw a plea on Facebook to help a single mom with two young children living in a motel. I donated $25 and forgot about it until the next day when my coworker, Jennifer, from Church Project, reached out. She couldn't convince the mom to put the children in foster care but could take the baby. She asked if I could take the two-year-old. I felt the Holy Spirit prompting me, and we agreed to a temporary eight-week commitment.

Ben: The boy instantly became part of our family. The girls loved him, and it was hard to give him back.

Kelly: When we took him in again, CPS got involved, and they encouraged us to hang on to the kids. Their parents weren't making progress, and the children weren't safe. We decided to fight for the kids in court, and that's when our House Church really rallied around us.

Our House Church supported us financially, providing more than just diapers and meals. Lorraine from our House Church even sold salsa to help with legal fees. At first, I wanted to handle it alone, but I realized it was the church's responsibility to care for orphans. I put the salsa fundraiser on Facebook, and my college roommate in New Zealand sent money. Friends of hers bought salsa, and a stranger gave us $500. We ended up raising $10,000, covering all our legal fees. It was a powerful reminder of the body of Christ coming together, and I'll never forget it.

THE PORTER FAMILY

My name is Kyle Lackey, and my family and I have been attending Church Project for a little over five years. From the beginning of our relationship, my wife and I knew adoption would be part of our future. As we got to know more people who had fostered and adopted, our hearts were moved from international adoption to domestic adoption, specifically foster care.

We began taking the necessary classes and doing everything required to get licensed to foster. Toward the end of that, we met a little boy named RJ, who was about 3 or 4 weeks old at the time. He had wild, curly hair and was super sweet, and we immediately felt a special place in our hearts for him.

Nine months later, I was approached by another member of our church who asked if we could take RJ in. I called Lisa, and before I could finish the sentence, she said, *Absolutely. Let's go get him.* So, we got involved and initiated the transfer. He came to live with us at nine months old — and he never left.

RJ was actually the third Church Project family he lived with. Normally, kids in foster care move from home to home, but looking back, it's amazing to see God's providence and His hand in this situation.

I don't think everyone is called to foster or adopt, but I do believe everyone is called to care for the orphan. For our family, that meant fostering and adoption. For others in our story, it meant helping with background checks to babysit, offering emotional support, or walking alongside us.

KYLE LACKEY

Absolutely gorgeous. Just the way she carried herself, her confidence. As soon as we made eye contact, there was something about her that captivated me. I knew I had to get to know her. It wasn't love at first sight, but it didn't take long for me to fall in love. There was excitement, a freshness, as we took on life together. We were both so engrossed in our careers — me, working at the sports clinic, focused on looking the part in the gym.

I never saw the betrayal coming. I thought everything was great in our marriage, but I began getting attention from other women, and simple conversations turned into emotional, then physical relationships. This went on for years.

In June 2018, Jen found out. She confronted me, and I partially confessed. It felt like my heart was ripped out. It was the most painful moment of my life. I received a text from a doctor I used to work with, recommending a 16-week marriage counseling course. We completed the first 8-9 weeks, and during a check-in, the counselor asked, *If you were standing before God right now, how would you feel?* I knew I wasn't being completely honest with Jen, and that was hard to admit.

That night, sitting in the garage at midnight, Jen came out, sat next to me, and prayed over us. Despite my heartache, there was a peace that only God could provide. I realized that God had poured grace through me to offer forgiveness to Josh, even though my heart was still hard. It was all Him.

I knew then that we could make it through this together. Moving forward required us to both fully commit. We worked on ourselves, but most importantly, we worked on our relationship with God. We joined a House Church, and now, two years later, we host one, with Josh even Pastoring. It's amazing to see how far we've come and how God has worked in us. I've learned that you can't do it alone. When you let go and let God, life becomes so much better.

JOSH & JENN BROWN, HOUSE CHURCH PASTOR & WIFE

I didn't know things could be wrong until junior high. Life was good — both at home and in my community at church. But the summer before seventh grade, two of my friends died in a car accident. It was the moment I realized the world wasn't what I thought — it was hard and bad things happened. Then in eighth grade, a friend of mine with a heart condition died right next to me in class. I hadn't experienced anything like this, and it left me feeling lost and overwhelmed.

I entered high school depressed, not knowing how to process all the pain. I didn't understand that what I was feeling was normal. Despite this, I continued volunteering at church, even leading worship on Wednesday nights. But when I came home, I didn't want to wake up the next day. I was praying, *God, please take this away. I don't understand why I'm here, but I feel lonely and lost.*

In the summer of 2018, I was volunteering with high school students when one of them, Matt, pulled me aside. He said, *I think you know God can heal you. You don't understand why He hasn't, but you don't believe He wants to.* His words hit me. I wasn't letting God do anything for me — I thought I had to earn it, thinking if I was good enough, God would take away my depression. But that's not how grace works. God doesn't wait for us to be perfect; He comes to us as we are, broken, and heals us.

It was hard, and it took time. I still struggle with depression and have bad days. But what I want people to know is that God loves you, sees your brokenness, and wants to meet you there. Some days, I still wish God would take away my depression, but I know He's working. I have a deep desire to help others, to show them my brokenness and tell them why I need a Savior. I can point to my need for Christ because I'm broken, and so are they.

One day, God will take away all that's not of Him. If we were perfect, we wouldn't need a Savior. But thank God we do, because He saves us and rebuilds us from the inside out.

JAMES DAVIS

We weren't sure if we could have biological kids, and I wanted to adopt. So, on our seventh wedding anniversary, we began the process to bring home our daughter, Zoe, from China. A year later, we found out we were pregnant with our oldest daughter, Aurelia. We were thrilled to have two kids, both one year old, and we thought adoption was so wonderful, we decided to do it again. Six months after bringing Zoe home, we started the adoption process from Ethiopia, but three days later, I found out I was pregnant with our son, Zadok.

The Ethiopia adoption process started quickly, but then it slowed down drastically. In April 2017, the Prime Minister suspended all international adoptions, leaving us devastated. Parents and adoption agencies petitioned in Washington, and a letter from 122 senators and congressmen helped change things. However, our case stalled again when our agency shut down. That's when the real struggle began. We went to Ethiopia, and after overcoming many obstacles, we finally met our daughter. At first, she was terrified, screamed, and wouldn't even look at us. But even though she didn't want us, we kept falling more in love with her. She was our child, even though we had only seen a picture of her for a year and a half.

When she was ripped out of my arms, it was devastating. But two months later, we returned to Ethiopia to complete the process and finally brought her home. When we landed in Houston and went through immigration, we couldn't believe it — she was home after five long years, and she was ours. Nothing could change that.

The obstacles we faced in Ethiopia seemed unmovable, but with the support of our House Church and Church Project, our community prayed with us, and things began to move. We literally watched God move mountains. The journey was incredibly hard, but I'm so thankful for the amazing community we had and for seeing God work in such powerful ways. It's a testimony we can now share with others.

ERIEK & LAURA HULSEMAN,
HOUSE CHURCH PASTOR & WIFE

Before coming to Church Project, I was lost, living one day at a time with no purpose. I had no regard for anyone, including myself, and was ready to throw everything away. I almost lost my family — my wife was about to leave with my children. I was a raging alcoholic and drug addict, hurting everyone around me.

Church Project gave me purpose. It opened my eyes to the goodness of people and how I can make a difference. I got my family back, cut off toxic friends, and gave up drinking and using. I now focus on work and taking care of my family.

Giving my life to Jesus changed me in ways I can't describe. The way I carry myself, walk, and talk has all transformed. I owe it all to Church Project. This is my forever home.

RYAN GARNER

I remember my mom would intentionally spend quiet moments with me, like when we'd sit in lawn chairs, soak up the sun, and she always made sure I knew I was wanted. One weekend, we went to the Houston Rodeo, which she pushed for, even though I didn't want to go. She stayed with me after the concert, and that was the worst day of my life. My mom passed away suddenly in her sleep, very unexpectedly. She was healthy, and I was the one to find her. In that instant, I was overwhelmed with grief, shame, regret, and anger at God for not giving me sweeter final moments with her.

In the midst of my loss, every single person in my House Church reached out to me. They texted, called, listened to me cry, made meals for my family, and even paid hundreds of dollars to cover my rent so I could take a month off work. One couple even paid for 12 trauma counseling sessions, an investment over a thousand dollars. I never felt alone. The love I received didn't make sense and wasn't expected, yet these people, led by God, did things that showed His heart for me.

Through their actions, God revealed Himself to me. He used my House Church to care for me, showing me that He is passionate about taking care of those who can't take care of themselves. At times, I couldn't even get out of bed, but someone paid for a cleaner because I was too broken to move. This experience showed me the power of community and the truth behind the saying, *To have a friend, be a friend.* God's love was made real through the tangible support of His people. It was the most real moment of my life.

DESARAE BALERIO

Chris: I didn't grow up going to church. I always knew there was something more, but I couldn't figure out what. I met my wife Amanda, who always wanted me to go to church, but our conversations often ended in arguments because I was stubborn. I thought something drastic would have to happen for me to believe. One night, at 3:30 a.m., I had a strange dream and woke up telling Amanda I was dying. I asked her to call 911.

Amanda: When he said he was dying, it didn't hit me until I was on my way to the hospital. I thought, What if I never see him again? How could I not love him enough to push for him to find Jesus? I begged God, *I'm sorry. If you give me another chance, I won't squander it.* At the hospital, Chris was awake and told me, *My brain is bleeding,* then cried in pain. The doctors sedated him. No wife should have to see her husband intubated and unconscious. I prayed over him.

Chris: As I lay there, I knew I was here for a reason. I shouldn't have survived, but I did.

Amanda: I felt like God was saying, I got this. I got you, and I got him. It's going to be hard, but it's going to be okay. Through days of therapy and hospital visits, Chris kept telling me, *God did that. God did that.* I wanted him to know everything was God's work.

Chris: He's a patient, forgiving God, because He knew it would take me a while to come around.

Amanda: People say God won't give you more than you can handle, but we were brought to our knees.

Chris: I had been head coach for a long time, and one of my assistant coaches, who had been coming to Church Project for years, invited us. We finally came, and halfway through Jason's sermon, I nudged Amanda and said, *This is where we're supposed to be.*

Amanda: We joined a House Church, which met many needs we didn't even know we had. Ron and Alan really connected with Chris. Last July, he was baptized.

CHRIS & AMANDA TATE, HOUSE CHURCH HOSTS

I was raised in a home that, looking back, wasn't really a home. My dad was strict and abusive, my mom unavailable, and as the oldest, I became responsible for my siblings. I believed I had to behave perfectly to earn my parents' love, and that carried over to my view of God. When my mom was diagnosed with cancer, we flew her back to Cambodia, where she passed away a few months later. My sister also passed away suddenly, and I wasn't with her when she died. Both losses felt incredibly unfair, and I didn't get to say goodbye.

After all the trauma, I coped by pretending everything was fine. I smiled through my pain, kept busy with work, school, and church, but deep down, I wasn't okay. By 2019, I hit a breaking point and started therapy. That's when I saw Church Project's GriefShare group. God began peeling away layers of pain I hadn't realized I was carrying. I realized I had never properly grieved my dad, still alive but emotionally absent.

Before, I would have tried to make people feel better quickly, but now I understood the importance of grieving. Jesus wept, and that's how we're meant to respond to loss. Seeing friends in House Church grieve, I knew I couldn't sit still. God didn't allow me to go through this pain for nothing. If you never allow yourself to feel the grief, you can't truly be present for others in their darkness. As the body of Christ, we're meant to sit with each other, even in uncomfortable moments. We are called to be there for one another.

DEBORA SHANLEY

I knew the Lord from a young age. My mom was obedient, setting an example with her devotions at the kitchen table. I was a good kid, an athlete, and attended youth group. But when my dad left when I was 12, things got rough. I made some poor choices, and by 16, I found myself pregnant. I chose adoption for my child. Lying in bed one night, I thought, I'm the problem. But then I heard God say, You have a purpose, and I have a plan for you.

I got on fire for the Lord, married right out of high school, and had three children. For the first 10 years, things were good. But gradually, my husband stepped away from church, community, and accountability. The marriage declined into alcoholism and infidelity. After 20 years, I was left feeling abandoned. My youngest son, 16 at the time, chose to stay with his father, which was unhealthy. A year later, he tragically took his own life.

People often ask me how I'm not a puddle on the floor. The answer is the Holy Spirit, who comforts me, saying, Kelly, I'm here, and I'm all you need. I can take anything broken and make beauty from it. Knowing who Jesus is and the sacrifice He made for me, taking on every sin — mine and others' — is what keeps me grounded. It brings me comfort and knocks me flat every time. In my darkest moments, I return to the truth: He died for me. He did it for everyone, past, present, and future.

KELE PANDOLFE

I was drinking, smoking, and living a chaotic life. We hung out with neighbors who were all using drugs, and everything felt like it was on a path to destruction. One night, my five-year-old son Timmy asked me what happens when we die, and I had no answer. That scared me. I started surrounding myself with Christians and joined a mom group, which led me to meet my friend Lindsay. But soon, I fell back into addiction and started taking pills. After a long drive to San Antonio for work, I overdosed on fentanyl. Andy didn't make it; he died in the hotel that night, and I barely made it home.

The next day, I still had fentanyl in my pocket. I overdosed again when I got home and ended up in the hospital, struggling to breathe. For days, I was in and out of consciousness with low oxygen levels. During that time, our House Church Pastor was always there. It was then that I truly experienced the grace of God. I'd heard of grace before, but this was different — the entire church poured out grace, and the transformation in my life was so powerful that I knew it could only be Jesus.

Our family has completely transformed. We both dropped out of school, I'd been to prison, and we were addicted to drugs. But now, we have a beautiful family and kids who love Jesus. Baptizing my own children was the perfect ending to this story.

TIM STRIKER

I've been married for 25 years and have an amazing daughter, who's a true blessing. Last June, I wasn't feeling well, chalking it up to menopause, but it only got worse. After returning from California, I ended up in the ER, where tests revealed something serious. The doctor told me I needed to see an oncologist immediately. I met Dr. Lee, who did more exams and a CAT scan. She sat me down and said, *Tanya, you have cancer.*

In that moment, I experienced a peace I couldn't explain. I had always heard of the peace the Bible talks about, but this was different. It wasn't easy for my family, though. My daughter couldn't even come into my room, and Chris struggled to stay strong. My verse that kept me grounded was Philippians 1:6: *Being confident of this one thing, that He who started a good work in you will complete it until the day of Jesus Christ.*

I had a full hysterectomy, followed by chemo every 21 days. In the infusion lab, I saw others struggling, and my heart broke for them. After a PET scan, Dr. Lee sat down with me and said, *This is a miracle.* She told me, *When I opened you up, I didn't think you would live to see your next birthday.* I replied, *That's the best birthday gift you could give me, since my birthday's tomorrow.*

If it wasn't for those little moments, step by step, knowing that God was right there with me, I don't know that I would've made it through like I did. He's real. He loves us. He wants us to cry out to Him. Thank God for no matter if it's one more breath, one more day, or another week—in my case, it's been another year. We still have to praise Him.

TANYA MEINERS

We had a pretty good life — comfortable, not rich, but content. Then, one day, my son got so worried about me vomiting that he called Taryn at work. She rushed home, and after I refused to go to the ER, she took my blood pressure, which was dangerously high. The doctors quickly diagnosed me with renal failure, and soon after, I was told I had multiple myeloma, a blood cancer.

As the doctor gave us the diagnosis, the room seemed to close in. I was overwhelmed with questions — What does this mean? What's the prognosis? How do we tell the kids? In that moment, the only thing that remained was the Holy Spirit, giving me peace. Though I grew up in church, I never made God a priority. I knew He was with me, but I was still resistant to fully surrender.

Later, after a serious setback with pneumonia, Taryn stayed connected with our House Church, and Pastor came to visit me in the hospital. That conversation and prayer deeply impacted me. The Holy Spirit's presence was undeniable. After he left, I felt a deep peace and knew it was time to rededicate my life to God and lead my family to do the same.

We had already started attending Church Project, and the community there helped us focus on becoming better followers of Jesus. This led to a powerful moment where our whole family got baptized together, publicly declaring our love for Jesus. It was one of the most special days of my life. Having a close relationship with the Lord has completely changed our lives.

CLAY SPEAKMAN

In late 2016, my husband and I found out we were expecting a baby due in August 2017. My pregnancy was full of excitement, but then Hurricane Harvey hit. The storm became a hurricane on August 24th, and my due date was the 28th. I called my doctor, and he told me to leave. We didn't know how bad it would be, but we had to leave our home just days before our son was due. It was terrifying.

Miraculously, everything came together. We drove north to a hospital that made space for us, and strangers sent gifts and supplies for the *hurricane baby*. Our home was damaged, but the nursery was ready. During that time, God's presence was undeniable. In the midst of chaos, He gave us peace and provided in ways we couldn't explain.

In 2019, we found out we were expecting another boy, due in May 2020. The joke was that this delivery would be a "cakewalk" compared to evacuating a hurricane, but nothing prepared us for the pandemic. COVID-

19 brought uncertainty, and there was no escape.

But by God's grace, the church was still the church. We leaned on our family, friends, and House Church more than ever. Their prayers became our peace. I couldn't have dreamed of bringing my boys into the world this way, but none of this surprised God. He promised He would be with us, and He has — faithfulness upon faithfulness.

KATIE KUGLER

Though my wife did her best raising our oldest daughter, I was an alcoholic husband and father. Over the years, we stuck with many House Churches and Sunday mornings. I had periods of sobriety, but also long stints of drunkenness. My family, growing with our second daughter, suffered from my verbal abuse and unpredictability. I was angry at God for giving me this affliction, unable to quit no matter how hard I tried. It took losing my health, family, and life to finally step aside and let God take control. God gave me the gift of desperation, and I took the offer to go to inpatient rehab, something I had always refused. My pride was broken, I was out of options, and I surrendered to His will.

Why does Church Project mean so much to me? Despite being in and out of addiction during the 10 years we've attended, the teachings I received from God's Word never left me. I'm now sober for 18 months, pursuing a Biblical Studies degree, and serving in many areas of church life. I'm no longer ashamed; I use my broken past to help others find His way.

The second, more miraculous reason, involves my daughters. While I was absent as the godly leader of our family, God worked through my wife to keep our girls on track with Jesus. My oldest has been part of the youth ministry for years, receiving love, mentorship, and support. The guilt I once carried for my parenting was replaced by God's grace, and my faith grew as I saw His presence in the church when I wasn't there. This has inspired me to help CP launch a recovery program to assist others struggling with addiction.

The more I walk in His ways and lead my family by example, the more I believe and trust that His ways are far better than mine. True peace and happiness have come from leaning on the Church Project and its example of how Christians should live. In this broken world, CP is a beacon of light, striving to live according to Scripture. CP's mission to glorify God and attract the world to Him through our example is something I'm proud to be part of. God bless our church!

DAVID CORGEY

Angela: I've always been nurturing, but I didn't know when I'd become a mom. I received advice that you don't have to give birth to be a mom. In May of 2020, I agreed to babysit for a foster child, and that's when I met him.

Joey: He reached out to me in a way that felt like he chose me. I wasn't often picked as a child, so it hit me deeply. When they asked about adoption, I didn't hesitate to say yes, even though I didn't know why. It felt right, like I already knew his story and couldn't let him go through more pain. God seemed to say, *I've made your way, just walk it.*

Angela: In September, I found out I was pregnant. Even after a miscarriage in October, we still said yes to adoption. It wasn't the way we planned, but I knew God had a baby for us. Through it all, God showed His presence through our community, church, family, and even CPS and CASA advocates.

Joey: At Church Project, we shared our story during a greeting time, and someone immediately offered to pay all our legal fees. I've seen a lot of generosity, but this was beyond anything I expected.

Angela: On the day of the trial, I cried tears of joy, overwhelmed by God's faithfulness. I don't know what our future holds, whether we'll foster or adopt again, but we are trusting God. His providence has been with us through this whole journey.

JOEY & ANGELA CROSS

Our first year of marriage was great — traveling, relaxing by the pool, and talking about expanding our family. In March 2020, we were thrilled by our first positive pregnancy test, but a week later, I started bleeding. At our eight-week appointment, the doctor confirmed there was no baby. That loss was painful, but the thought of having motherhood ripped away from me hurt even more.

We bought our first home in June and were excited to start a family. In August, we got another positive test, and this time, there was a baby. At our six-week checkup, we saw a heartbeat, but by seven weeks, the doctor couldn't find it. She told us we would need to terminate the pregnancy. The medicine partially worked, and I was left crying, *Did I just kill my baby?* After a second dose, the contractions began, and Tyler held my hand as we prayed and questioned God in the middle of the pain.

A friend told me about Waiting In Hope, and though I was skeptical, it turned out to be so much more than I expected. The support I received softened my heart, and I began to see a bigger picture. In 2021, after returning from our Florida trip, I took another test — positive. At our eight-week appointment, the doctor showed us a heartbeat. We were finally going to be parents. Our son, Andrew Marshall, was born on Thanksgiving Day at 37 weeks.

Through our losses, Tyler and I grew stronger as a couple, and our faith in God deepened. We became more involved with Church Project and found our House Church, which has been such a blessing. I don't know why our journey to parenthood was filled with heartbreak, but I know that after the storm, God brings a beautiful rainbow.

BRITTANY CASE

Since I was little, I had a plan for my life. Instead of trusting God, I was presenting Him with my plan and asking Him to bless it. After a few years of marriage, we decided it was time to have a baby. But months turned into years with no success. We went through testing and saw multiple doctors, and were told that conceiving naturally was unlikely. Meanwhile, everyone around me seemed to be getting pregnant easily, and I felt alone.

People from my House Church told me about Waiting in Hope, so I reached out to Brandi, one of the leaders. She called me immediately and invited me to come. When I attended, it was a beautiful, supportive group. During that time, I was also going through a study called The Heart of Hannah, about Hannah's prayers during her infertility. What struck me was that the study ended before she got pregnant — it focused on her heart, her waiting, and her complete surrender to God. It wasn't about her getting pregnant; it was about how we wait.

At that point in my journey, this is exactly what I needed. God knew that. He wanted me to fully let go and trust Him. I had never truly surrendered everything to Him until that moment. I'm thankful for every tear and every part of that journey because it deepened my relationship with Him and taught me that His plans are far better than mine, whether they align with my expectations or not.

CYDNEY HUCKINS

Hi, I'm Andrew Howorth, and this is my story. Growing up, I didn't have a relationship with God. By my teens, I was focused on girls and pushing boundaries. I met my future wife, and we started our relationship selfishly, being physical. After 15 years of marriage, we had two kids, nice cars, and money, but no happiness. Material things weren't enough, and I wasn't enough for my wife. I lived a life of sexual immorality, including pornography, which eventually came to light. The guilt and shame overwhelmed me, and I thought my marriage was over.

I wanted to fix things but couldn't. One night, my wife and I told our kids that things weren't good, and I thought there was no hope. But God placed godly men in my life who gave me hope, reminding me that if I did my part, God would do His. Despite others telling me to leave, I wanted to save my marriage, so we saw a Christian counselor. I went in angry, but the counselor helped me see that my selfish desires were destroying our relationship.

We started attending Church Project, and though I initially went to check a box, it was there that I realized the power of God's grace. I heard a message that spoke directly to me about sexual immorality, and I knew we could be saved. Even after serving divorce papers, I felt hope.

My life changed dramatically. It wasn't an act. God transformed me, and now, I'm selfless and caring. I see my wife and kids as a gift. I never imagined this change, but it's only by God's grace. Our marriage is now centered on God's love. I've seen firsthand how my wife forgave me, showing the grace of God. Life is just completely changed because of God.

ANDREW HOWORTH, HOUSE CHURCH PASTOR

My dad loved the Lord and always dreamed of being a Pastor. He lived that calling his whole life. Growing up, my brother and I got into trouble, and my dad often rebuked us with Bible verses. One day, while my dad was at work, he had a seizure, and the doctors couldn't explain why. After a second opinion, they found an aggressive brain tumor with a very low chance of survival. Despite this, I prayed fervently, believing God could heal him.

On the day of the surgery, I expected a miracle — a call saying the tumor had disappeared. But instead, my dad underwent an eight-hour surgery. I was confused. I knew God could heal him, but why wasn't He choosing to do so? The tumor kept growing, and despite radiation and chemo, my dad's condition worsened. We continued to pray for a miracle, but one day, I felt the Lord telling me to change my prayer. Instead of praying for healing, I prayed for my family to learn to live without my dad.

In October, my dad passed away and went to be with the Lord. While this wasn't the outcome I wanted, I know God is still good — not because of the healing or circumstances, but because through this, my dad found salvation. I know he's in heaven, and one day, I'll see him again. While God is a God of miracles and healing, the greatest gift He gives us is salvation.

WHITNEY HUGHES

Some of you may know a little of our story, but our daughter Ellie was inpatient at a children's hospital for almost 8 months this past year waiting on a heart transplant due to heart failure. We had only attended CP a handful of times before she was admitted to the hospital, and didn't personally know many from the church at all, but the outpouring of love and generosity was truly humbling and carried us through very dark times. Our house church family led by the Monsivaiz's and pastors, Trevor and Calvin, invested in us and our journey, we never felt alone. We also couldn't believe that so many people who we had never met in person would pray so faithfully, give so sacrificially and love us so well! Church Project has truly been the hands of feet of Jesus in our lives and we are forever grateful!

DYLAN & JAMI CRANE

Rachel: I always wanted to adopt, but didn't know what that would look like. I wasn't sure I could have biological children, so adoption seemed like something I'd do one day.

Chuck: The idea resurfaced when we talked about the need for foster families. At that moment, I learned kids were spending 3 or 4 days in CPS offices before being placed. It hit me hard, and I was on board.

Rachel: We initially didn't want to adopt but felt called to support biological families and ensure kids were safe while their parents got their lives together.

Chuck: About two years in, my heart started to change. I realized how difficult it was to say goodbye to the kids every time they went home.

Rachel: Then, we got a call to take two kids for 24 hours. Lexi and her brother came, and shortly after, Lexi needed a new home. She stayed with us for nine months. We thought we were on track to adopt her, but then we got the news she was going back home. That was really hard.

A few months later, we were placed with five kids under five, but we lost our house and had to move. It was tough, but we were provided with a house that fit our needs way better. God's faithfulness of sending people to serve us, and sending family members to come and be that support for us, was incredible. He surrounded us with people who loved our kids. And time and time again, when we thought, *This is too much, this is too hard,* God brought people alongside us.

Chuck: Having a core group of people to do life with and invest in each other has been such a blessing. Being here at Church Project and getting plugged into a House Church has been absolutely fantastic.

THE PANKRATZ FAMILY

Keith: We grew up in the same church in a small town in Oklahoma. We started dating when I was a senior in high school.

Jessica: After we married, people immediately asked, *When are you having kids?* Keith always replied, *In five years,* and I thought he was just making up a number. I'm a big planner, so I decided I'd have a baby in January to take the maximum time off from teaching. We got pregnant right away, but I didn't know I had a blood clotting issue, and we lost two babies that year. In January, we got pregnant again, and our baby arrived on my first due date, four days late.

Keith: I read Adopted for Life by Russell Moore, which deepened my understanding of the theology of adoption.

Jessica: We both talked about adoption and biological kids, and soon we brought two boys home. It was crazy at first — they didn't speak English, could run away, and destroy things. The whole adoption journey changed us. Marriage helped me be selfless, parenting helped me love others more, and adopting helped me understand God's love for me. We love our boys just like we love our biological child, Avery. It's a reflection of how God sees us through Jesus.

Keith: To me, adoption shows God's love, grace, and mercy. He chose me, not because of anything I did, but because He chose me.
KEITH & JESSICA KOTRLA

I was talented enough to manufacture my own goodness and satisfy myself, instead of relying on God. I graduated and went to A&M, where the first year and a half was great. But in the last year and a half, everything fell apart. I lost everything I had built, faced more failures than successes, and became isolated again. Eventually, I became homeless, lost my car, and a relationship that meant a lot to me.

In my depression, I turned to alcohol to self-medicate. I told myself I was a functional alcoholic, but really, I was a dysfunctional person. I looked in the mirror one day and hated the person I saw so much that I didn't recognize myself. In a moment of desperation, I attempted suicide. Just before I went through with it, I cried out to God, wanting Him to understand my pain. And clear as day, I heard His voice say, Your life is worth living.

I knew then that I had to make a lot of changes. I wasn't perfect, and I still made mistakes, but I began to depend on God in all things. I realized that just walking around isn't truly living — living means understanding that God has an identity and purpose for me. This life is His, and everything I do should be for Him. God made me new, and I wouldn't trade that for anything.
ERIC KNIGHT, HOUSE CHURCH PASTOR

Support Groups: CHURCHPROJECT.ORG/CARE

TEN

Kids & Students

In 15 years of Church Project, we've seen young kids graduate high school and Fifty6 students grow up, get married and start having their own families. Multiple generations have cycled through Church Project, revealing a unique view into God's faithfulness over a local body of believers. We have seen Project Kids, Fifty6, and Project Students lead countless kids and students to the gospel and pastor them in their knowledge, obedience and love to God.

Each week, kids and students gather to learn God's Word, worship Jesus and share time together. Throughout the year, they gather at retreats and camps and big, fun moments where they are create real friendships, experience what it's like to serve and meet needs, and increase their faith.

We dedicate our kids to God, committing to raise them within the church and under the authority of Scripture. We serve once a month in Project Kids where we disciple one another's kids to love and follow Jesus. And we have dedicated Student Group Leaders who live life with our students through many years, discipling them to belong with other students, believe in Jesus, and become who God intended them to be.

These are some of the stories from parents, students and leaders who have shared in these moments, serve with their time and care deeply about the next generation of the Church.

———————

Being part of Church Project has deeply impacted our family. We've built a strong sense of community as our children have grown from Project Kids to Project Students, with one now a young adult. As the Project Kids Pastor, my connection to this community has deepened. I have the privilege of discipling children and witnessing their growth and joy firsthand. I take great pleasure in partnering with parents to guide their children in faith, planting seeds of knowledge about who Jesus is and helping them find their identity in Him. I never take this responsibility lightly.

Building relationships while serving in Project Kids is both unique and rewarding. I value collaborating with those who understand the significance of leading and nurturing even the youngest hearts. After 11 years at Church Project, I've seen children grow into young adults, many of whom now serve in Project Kids. It's inspiring to witness an entire generation of Christ followers maturing and recognizing the profound impact Church Project has had on their lives. I'm excited to see the influence they'll have on the world!

TARA EDWARDS, PROJECT KIDS PASTOR

Growing up, I lived without purpose. I was passionate about golf, fun, and girls, but not about Jesus. I loved music and promoted bands for dances, but a disagreement with a friend ended with him punching me in the face. That moment led me to meet a Campus Crusade for Christ leader who invited me to a meeting. There, he shared the gospel, and it hit me like a lightning bolt. Everything I was living for seemed unimportant.

God has been so good to me. He gave me a wife who has been a godly mother, and three amazing kids: Stephanie, Melanie, and Gregory. Being a father has been the greatest joy and sometimes the greatest pain of my life. But it's the most rewarding experience, even as I look back and regret not spending more time with my kids when they were young.

I often tell young professionals that your kids don't care about your career. They just want you in their lives. The greatest regret you can have is realizing you didn't invest enough in your children. Paul reminds us to focus on the unseen, the eternal, rather than the things that are temporary — wealth, status, or possessions.

I'm incredibly proud of my kids, that they love Jesus, want to serve

God, and have grown up with a deep faith. The greatest reward is walking through life with Jesus. He is the center, the only game in town. He is life to me.

TRACE HOWARD, ELDER

We were encouraged by the sermons at CP to serve in the church. Tara convinced us to serve in Project Kids. Initially, we weren't eager, since our kids are grown, but over time it's become something we look forward to each month. We've been blessed to teach the gospel to the children and build community with other volunteers and the Project Kids staff. A few months later, when Jerry needed life-saving surgery, Tara, the Pastoral staff, and our House Church supported us every step of the way. The prayer and support they provided were unlike anything we'd ever experienced. CP has become more than just our church; it's become family.

JERRY & CHRISTY COOK

I have had the honor of serving in Project Kids for about 8 years. It has blessed me and my family so much! I love to be able to have a small part in discipling the youngest members of our church. It is so much fun to help them absorb God's Word and hide it in their hearts. I have gotten to enjoy serving at Kids Camp, Kids Week, and many other children's ministry events. This ministry is shaping the future church into Christ followers, and I am happy to be a part of it!

ASHLEY LEE, HOUSE CHURCH HOST

When my husband and I first started attending Church Project, our oldest daughter was almost one. We immediately knew we had found our church home. After a few months, we felt called to serve in the children's ministry, especially with a child of our own. As CP grew, we continued serving in ProjectKids until our middle daughter, Remley, finished fourth grade. When our daughters reached the age to attend church camp, I felt called to serve more, so I attended my first camp with all three daughters. I served as a counselor at several summer camps until Covid hit. After 12 years, Mike and I retired from ProjectKids, but I felt my time wasn't over. I returned to camp as a nurse's aide and transitioned to coaching the 9:00

service. Now, my oldest two daughters serve alongside me, and my youngest can't wait for her turn. God placed a heart to serve in me, and His love for me and our church has helped raise our daughters with a heart of service. Serving together has led to life-long friendships, and we know God has used our gifts to share His love with children.

HEATHER WELCH

I started attending CP in 2015 and felt God prompting me to serve. I knew I was called to help where there was need, and the greatest need I saw was in Kid's Ministry. However, I kept finding reasons not to serve. After months of ignoring the conviction, I had a dream in February 2021. I dreamed I received a phone call asking, *Will you be serving in Kid's Ministry?* The call repeated three times, and when I woke up, I knew I couldn't ignore it any longer. That Sunday, I spoke to Tara and signed up to serve with Project Kids Jr.

Serving in the classroom was uncomfortable at first, but I knew it was where God called me, so I stayed. After a year, Gretchen invited me to become a PK Jr. Coach, where I could support others serving in ministry. Serving in Project Kids Jr. has taught me to step forward in obedience and serve cheerfully, reminding me that serving isn't about doing what I want, but sacrificially building up the church body. God has grown my selflessness, patience, faithfulness, and love, and I'm blessed to be part of the work He's doing. I pray I'll continue to say yes to His call the first time He invites me.

KIERSON FLETCHER

I've always wanted a believer's baptism, having only been baptized as an infant. When my six-year-old expressed interest in baptism after seeing it at church, her teacher suggested it was a good time to start the conversation. Over the next few weeks, we discussed baptism and its meaning, and she became eager to be baptized to show everyone she is a Christian. Her enthusiasm reminded me there was no time like the present. In October, my daughter and I were baptized together, and it's a memory we will cherish for eternity.

SARAH ARMSTRONG

Eight years ago, I started taking my grandkids to VBS at Church Project when they began asking questions about God. We decided it was time to attend church regularly, and starting with VBS was the best decision we made. I needed a place where my grandkids could grow in their faith, as well as emotionally, mentally, and physically, and Project Abilities has made that happen. I'm so thankful for the impact on Max's life.

Max, my oldest, was five when he first started VBS. He had been diagnosed with ADHD and was a handful, so I needed a place that would understand and support him. At 11, Max was diagnosed with autism, which wasn't a surprise. But through the loving support of the church, Max has made incredible strides. He's learned to manage his behavior, walk away from conflicts, and admit mistakes, which has been huge. We're still working through challenges, but the church's understanding and kindness have made all the difference.

Today, three of my grandkids have found a true home at Church Project, and I've found a great church family and wonderful friends, which has been a blessing through all the ups and downs.
DEBBIE ARNOLD

He was kind, gentle, and a hard worker. He looked like George Strait, wore his hat and starched jeans, and worked with horses and ropes when we were little. On July 11th, I received a text saying, *Dad's in the hospital.* My heart sank. I didn't know what was going on. When I got home, I called my stepmom and found out he had bladder cancer. He didn't want us to know, waiting until he had a plan.

The next morning, we learned his kidney function was worsening. I asked my House Church and Project Kids for prayer. Pastor John called to encourage me and asked if my dad was a believer. I wasn't sure. I knew he'd grown up in church and was proud of me for volunteering, but I didn't know if he'd called Jesus Lord.

I packed up and drove to Edna with my Bible. When I arrived, Dad looked like he was sleeping, with machines beeping around him. I sat by his bed, opened my Bible, and started reading. As I read John 3:8 about the wind and the Spirit, my dad opened his eyes, sat up, and looked at me with a face full of light. *Hi, Daddy, I love you*, I said. He replied, *Hi, baby.* I finished reading, saying *Amen.*

The undeniable presence of Jesus filled the room. I used to wonder what to say, unsure of myself. But now I know the world needs to hear that Jesus is here, and it's time to share that He loves you.

KACY NORRIS, CP STAFF

I was teaching a lesson about Zacchaeus being a sinner, and one of the kids said, *What's a sinner?* I explained, *A sinner is someone who doesn't follow God's commands.*

The child then said, *Well, I'm a sinner.* That was a powerful moment because admitting you're a sinner is the first step in coming to faith.

I've worked in adult ministry for a long time and seen a lot of fruit. But in seminary, one professor said, "These kids need someone other than their father to show them who Jesus is." That was a game-changer for me. I realized I needed to be part of children's ministry, so I shifted gears and began focusing on it.

There aren't many men in children's ministry because it's often seen as *unmanly.* Yet, if a big physical task needs doing, like digging a ditch, you'd see hundreds of men show up. But serving in children's ministry is just as important. Kids need to see male figures — other than their fathers — serving them. God, as a male figure, and Jesus, the Son, are essential models for them. That's why it's vital for men to serve in children's ministry.

When I switched from adult ministry to children's, it was a big shift, but it's incredibly rewarding. The impact on kids can last a lifetime. You may never know the full extent of it, but knowing you made a difference in even one child's life is huge. At Church Project, we have the opportunity every week to impact twenty, thirty, or even forty kids, and it's a blessing to be a part of their growth.

STEVE ECKHART

Kids are the next generation of Christ followers. In Project Kids, we teach children God's word and biblical principles to help parents instill faith that will carry them through life and be passed to future generations. Kids are curious, uninhibited, candid, and fun! They're the focus of our ministry, but volunteers are its strength. Volunteers are parents, grandparents, young

adults, teens, homeschool moms, dads, and whole House Churches serving together. They teach, encourage, lead teams, and disciple kids. Project Kids volunteers represent the whole body of Christ — parents, teens, young adults, and older generations — who make a difference by teaching kids to love and follow Jesus. Watching this vibrant, multi-generational community of volunteers investing in future generations is uplifting and a testament to the unity of the body of Christ.
GRETCHEN JONES, CP STAFF

I was nine months pregnant with our third son when I found a lump on Jacob's sternum, the size of an egg. I called the pediatrician, who was concerned but hesitant to mention cancer. We saw a doctor at Texas Children's Hospital, and the waiting room filled with children who had clearly undergone cancer treatments made it hit home. We were referred to a pediatric oncologist, but nothing was confirmed. The next days felt aimless. We prayed, struggling to ask God for healing, knowing we had to be prepared for Him not to answer as we hoped. That night, we broke down praying together, the hardest we've ever cried as a married couple.

Two weeks later, we returned to the hospital. As we were about to leave, a nurse ran out to get us. My heart skipped a beat, thinking the news was bad. But minutes later, the doctor came in and said, *It's not cancer. I don't know what it is, but it's not cancer.* That morning, the lumps started disappearing, and by evening, they were gone. Later that day, I gave birth to our third child.

I don't know why God chose to answer our prayer this way. It's not because we are more deserving than others who've lost children. This isn't a story about a miracle — it's about God growing a frail faith, showing a love so deep He would enter our fears and vulnerabilities just to take the test.
CHRIS & SUMMER LACY

My name is Chris Reece. My wife Kallie, our kids Mason and Mallory, and I have been attending Church Project for two years and are deeply connected to our House Church, which has become our family. For years, I applied for my dream job as an air traffic controller. In January, I received the call to attend the FAA Academy in Oklahoma City. In February, I moved there, leaving Kallie and the kids behind.

On Father's Day weekend, while preparing for my final week at the Academy, Mason tried to drink lighter fluid. I called 911 and rushed to Texas Children's Hospital, feeling completely helpless. The doctors couldn't tell us if he would survive, and the next 24 hours were filled with intense prayer, trusting God to heal him. By day seven, Mason was stable enough to be weaned from sedation. When he opened his eyes, it felt like seeing him born again. God had given me a second chance to be his mom. Mason had no burns or damage and was perfectly healthy.

Through this, I truly understood community. At Church Project, we talk about community, but experiencing it firsthand was life-changing. The love and support from our Church Project family was incredible and a true blessing.

CHRIS & KALLIE REECE

Church Project has been crucial in growing my faith. Growing up in a church rooted in legalism, I didn't realize how deeply it affected me until I came to Church Project and understood grace more fully. The Holy Spirit revealed this to me as we studied the book of John. I have found so much freedom in Christ and His grace, for which I am truly thankful.

The way we study scripture each week has taught me personal rhythms I've incorporated into my daily life. Jason's teaching and approach to scripture has modeled for me how to read and study effectively. Good.God. Gospel has also been a powerful tool, helping me share the gospel more intentionally. I've seen how much of a difference it makes and how God works over time, even when the results aren't immediate.

When I first came to Church Project, I didn't immediately join a House Church, but now I realize how much I missed. The community and friendships in my House Church are vital to me. Being part of a cross-generational group to study scripture and do life together is something I need. I love my House Church, and we enjoy serving together.

Serving in Project Kids has been a blessing. Watching kids worship Jesus and grow in their desire to love and follow Him is encouraging. We memorize and read scripture together, and learn about our ministry partners and service. After years in public education, I had become discouraged about future generations, but serving in Project Kids has shown me how much God is still working in the lives of our kids and students. I also love going through Good.God.Gospel with them.

I love Church Project — how involved we are in our city and with ministry partners, how we're a church of House Churches with strong community, and how we're committed to spreading the gospel locally and globally. I love how we love others as Jesus does, and I've personally experienced the love, support, and encouragement of Church Project through both hard and great seasons of life. I'm truly grateful.

LANEY GILLESPIE, CP STAFF

I began serving with students during a challenging time in my life. At the end of my tough freshman year, Calvin Taylor asked me to lead a mission trip to Alaska. I said yes without much thought, then panicked, unsure why I was going. I prayed for the Lord to reveal His purpose. By the end of the trip, God showed me my gifts and ignited a passion for student ministry.

Four years later, I'm still leading students, and it's the greatest honor of my life. This is a critical age where beliefs are foundational. Growing up in Scotland, I lacked examples of young people living for Jesus. When hard things came, I had no theology for suffering, which shook my faith. I want every student to know they are loved by God, created with purpose, and that following Jesus is worth everything, no matter the world's views.

Our students are searching for belonging and meaning. Every Monday, I see them find answers and invite friends. Trevor and I are seeing a ripple effect in our city. I've learned that when students are given opportunities, they exceed expectations. I've witnessed this on mission trips and by teaching students to disciple and connect to others. I encourage them with 1 Timothy 4:12: *Don't let anyone look down on you because you are young, but set an example for the believers.* I believe their impact can be significant from a young age. My hope for Project Students is that it remains a place of belonging, transformation, and bold faith. I'm excited to be a part of what's happening in Project Students.

BETH WATT, CP STAFF

I grew up in a small church until we had to move my 9th grade year.

We visited Church Project, and though I was nervous about joining a larger church, it immediately felt like home. At CP, I felt seen and loved, with people quickly encouraging and pushing me. I was given many service opportunities like mission trips, homeless ministry, and youth events, which tested and strengthened my faith. Church Project is the most important part of my life because it's where my family is. God gave me a place to be open and real with my struggles, questions, and victories. Through Church Project and Project Students, I found people who push me, love me, know me, and lead me both inside and outside of church.

SHAYLEE ABERNATHA

I've been attending Church Project for a year, consistently praying and seeking the Lord's guidance on where He wanted me to serve. I felt led to serve in the student ministry, leading 8th grade girls. As the year went on, I sensed God calling me out of my comfort zone, so I served at the students' summer camp. There, I built strong community with other leaders and led 10th grade girls, witnessing their hunger for the Lord. Though I never saw myself as a teacher, seeing God use me to further His kingdom was humbling. Shortly after, I was invited to lead 7th grade girls on Monday nights. It's been an honor to guide them, and I look forward to sharing my full testimony and seeing how God works in their lives.

ASHLEY BANDA, STUDENT GROUP LEADER

I started coming to Church Project almost two years ago. My family and I weren't having the best experience at our old church, especially me. I would go because I had to, sitting alone because I wasn't part of the group. The first few months at CP, I didn't make any friends, scared of being left out again. I started attending Monday Nights (mainly because my mom made me) and began to feel like people actually cared about me. Then I went to Encounter, and my eyes were opened. I always loved God, but I never had a real relationship with Him. Encounter made me realize how much God, this church, and my friends loved me. I began attending church every Sunday and Monday, and my relationship with Jesus and my friends deepened.

Things kept growing — until August, when my dad unexpectedly passed away. I never got a chance to say goodbye, and this devastated me. But I know I would have been in a much worse place without Jesus and Church Project. I was lost, angry, and sad. Thanks to my friends, and leaders Molly and Sam, I knew I had people who would support me through this difficult time. It's only been a few months, and I'm not fully healed, but I'm so grateful for the loving community at CP that has helped me grow in my relationship with Christ.

LORI WHATLEY

I've been fortunate to find family at Church Project. As a teenager, my parents don't regularly attend church with me, which has been a struggle. However, since 4th grade, I've been part of the Project Kids worship team (aka Glitter Squad). Over time, I've become more invested in Project Kids and have earned the trust to lead worship services. Leading kids in worship every week brings me the greatest joy. I wouldn't be where I am without my worship leader, Mrs. Kacy, who has always taught, loved, supported, and set an example for me. My worship team is made up of some of my best friends. My small group and leaders mean so much to me, and I wouldn't be who I am today without them. I feel incredibly blessed by the gifts the Lord has entrusted me with, even when life is hard. 1 Timothy 4:12: *Do not let anyone look down on you because you are young, but set an example for the believers in speech, in conduct, in faith, in love, and in purity.*

KYLIE BELLINI

I joined Church Project in the summer of 4th grade and started attending Fifty6, but I didn't have any friends and struggled to understand why I was there. I went mainly to play games and attend fun events, but didn't grasp what church meant. In 7th grade, I met my now student group leaders, Wyatt and Kyron. At the time, I didn't care much about learning about God, but everything changed when I went to the 2023 retreat. Surrounded by so many Christians who loved and cared for me, I felt something I had never felt before. After that, I started attending Project Students and Sunday services, listening to the sermons and worship. I began to feel the Holy Spirit and that's when my faith truly started growing. In February, I was baptized with my friends and family supporting me.

I've also attended student retreats like camp in New Mexico and the Austin trip, which changed my perspective on many things. Some of my family and friends aren't Christians, and it's hard to accept that they don't believe in God. But I'm excited for the coming years in Project Students and can't wait to grow my faith even more. I'm grateful for my brothers in my group and my leaders, and look forward to spending these years with them.

COLIN THOMAS

My family started attending Church Project in 2013, and I've grown up in Project Kids and Project Students. I'm grateful to have been part of such an amazing small group and have learned so much from them. I've built long-lasting relationships with the girls in my group and our leaders, Taylor and Angela. Even though we've all graduated and are now in college, we still meet up multiple times a year and keep in touch regularly. This past summer, I had the privilege of being the Project Students intern. It was incredible to return and serve the ministry that served me. Watching students grow in their faith throughout the summer was a blessing. I'm thankful for the opportunity to be part of such an amazing ministry in these ways over the years.

AUDREY EDWARDS

Being part of Church Project has been essential for our family. It's not just a place to worship, but a community that has blessed our children's lives. Project Students has provided amazing opportunities to learn about serving and put it into practice. They have supportive leaders and mentors who help them grow in their faith and as individuals.

Project Students has been more than a support system for our kids; it's also supported us as parents, providing valuable parenting tools. Our children have been blessed with mission trips, summer camps, serving weekends like Encounter, leadership opportunities in Project Kids, and more. Through it all, they've formed Godly friendships that will last a lifetime. We are forever grateful for Church Project and the impact Project Students has had and continues to have on our children. Project Students, we love you!

MICHAEL & RO BENIGNUS

Growing up at Church Project has shaped me into who I am because of the people who serve in Project Kids, Fifty6 Students, and Project Students. Every person serving once a month has a huge impact on kids and students who will one day be in college, surrounded by diverse backgrounds.

Being built up by the body of believers is something kids and students don't fully realize until they're living on their own, needing to provide for themselves spiritually, emotionally, and physically. Seeing people passionate about returning to Christ's vision for the church — and committed to helping the next generation know and follow Jesus — has been powerful.

I've been part of this since 1st grade, and as I've grown, I've had the chance to lead both kids and high school students. Our faith is built on the continuous loop of discipleship that's been passed down for 2,000 years. Serving at Church Project has shaped me into who I am, and we all get to be part of it.

PORTER JOHNSON

Church Project has provided a place for our whole family to serve and be involved. We moved to Spring two years ago, and God led us to CP on our second Sunday in town. The next night, my high-school girls went to Students, and that Wednesday, we joined the House Church closest to our home. We jumped right in, found community, and a church home. Whatever CP is doing, my children want to be there. The more we serve at CP (in Jr, Kids, Fifty6, Students, greeting, coffee, and House Church), the more we love this community of God's people. I am blessed to see our whole family invest in this place and thrive.

SARAH HUCKABY

I love performing. I grew up in a dance studio, performing shows about God, but also battling headaches. My mom, the school principal, suffered from them too. Recently, my migraines became debilitating — throwing up daily, waking up blind, nausea, dizziness. Some days, I couldn't get out of bed. My mom, despite her pain, would power through, working in small bursts before resting. The migraines were so bad, I started passing out at the studio. The hardest part wasn't quitting dancing — it was knowing I had to. I was mad at God, asking: *Why am I like this? Why am I quitting something I'm doing for you?* I began to shut down emotionally. One day, my mom pushed me to talk, and I said the scariest thing any parent could hear: *I can't talk about the future because I don't see myself in it.*

We got me into counseling and took it one step at a time. My dance teacher, who had undergone multiple brain surgeries for Chiari malformation, understood and prayed over me when I struggled. She reminded me, "You don't have to find your identity in your dance. Find it in Christ." At 17, I learned what many don't realize until later: Sometimes, you need to go through hard things to become who you're meant to be. There's hope beyond the pain. Even if your story isn't finished, you can still make an impact. You can still smile through it.

RYLIE PORTER

I am a seventh-grade student at Church Project, and my family has been attending for 9 years. During my time at CP, I've gone from not being able to read the Bible to reading it daily and giving my life to God. CP has shaped me into the person God wants me to be. I've had great experiences through Project Kids, Fifty-Six, and Project Students. I've found my closest friends here and am committed to bringing my school friends into this environment. There's a place for everyone at CP, with events and groups for all ages and stages of life. I can't imagine life without my church family. Thank you, Church Project, for giving me a place to thrive and truly belong.

ARIA KAMERER

I have been in Church Project for over 10 years. This is where I found the lord in my life and accepted him into my heart. It on one of the few things that I look forward to when I come home. I'm extremely proud to call Church Project my home.

HALEY HOWORTH

I believe God directed my family to Church Project at a critical time. A few weeks after starting, our son was diagnosed with a rare medical condition. The support from the student department and Home Church has been a pillar of strength. They've regularly laid hands on him and prayed for him.

We've witnessed God's faithfulness as doctors changed his diagnosis from needing invasive brain surgery to a less invasive solution. We are deeply grateful for the love and support of the Church Project family as we continue our son's healing journey.

ALEX ARAYA

Beth: With four boys at home, it's always loud, fun, and never a dull moment. We noticed Elijah had a speech delay, which we were told would improve as he grew. But when he started kindergarten, things worsened. He had 15 to 20 meltdowns a day. The principal suggested an evaluation for autism, and I was shocked. I knew nothing about autism and was in disbelief. It felt like we had to relearn our child, as everything started making sense. It was isolating — being in a room full of people yet feeling alone. We didn't know how to help Elijah, and we longed for a place where our whole family could connect and hear the truth of the gospel from others, not just us. I couldn't be the only one speaking truth into them.

Troy: We wanted our kids to be part of something bigger, and that's what Projectability helped them do.

Beth: Elijah started seventh grade sitting at the back. Over the year, he moved up to sitting with his group, eventually worshiping front row, wholeheartedly, with loud music and all. A month ago, we talked late into the night about what we learned at church, and Elijah committed his life to Christ. Now, we're talking about baptism.

Troy: Seeing my kids plugged in and involved is the most incredible feeling, and I know that impact will last a lifetime.

THE PARISH FAMILY

The only memories I have of my parents together are of them fighting. As a child, I felt scared and longed for something I couldn't name. My parents had a 50/50 split, but at 15, my relationship with my dad was severed, causing immense pain. High school was dark for me, and there were times I felt the world would be better off without me.

Then a friend invited me to Church Project. She saw me struggling and handed me a card, inviting me to join her at ten. I remember telling my parents about this church in a warehouse, and they thought I was crazy. But when I showed up, the worship washed over me, and I felt peace. I joined the student group and House Church, where Pastors poured into me. That's when I truly started my relationship with Jesus, and my life changed.

I even had a coach tell me I was glowing. After high school, my mom and stepdad divorced, which sent me spiraling again. I prayed for a friend, and God brought me my husband. Eight weeks ago, we had our daughter, Lyla. The first night we brought her home, God broke open my heart. There was a deep hurt I never thought could be healed, but God mended it.

Seeing my husband with our daughter reminded me of the healing I never thought possible. I'm forever grateful that someone took the time to invite me to church. Without that, I wouldn't be the wife or mom I am today, and I don't know if I'd even be here. It meant everything.

KENDALL PHILIPS, FORMER STUDENT
& STUDENT GROUP LEADER

I grew up in a small town in Spain. My parents divorced when I was three, which was tough for my sister and me. It was hard, and I didn't really understand it at the time. A couple of years ago, I decided to study in the U.S. for a year. Texas seemed cool, especially the Cowboys, and I quickly felt at home. After just two days, I was already close to my host family. We became best friends, and I felt like part of the family.

Back home, my grandma went to church, but young people didn't. If you went to church, they'd make fun of you. My host family took me to church every Sunday, Monday, and Wednesday. At first, it was overwhelming. But during a retreat, when we worshipped and Trevor spoke about the lost son, something shifted in me. I started crying, feeling something I had never felt before — like God was moving in my heart. Over time, I noticed more and more moments like this, and I could see God working in my life.

I had many conversations where I felt that God had brought me here for a reason, that switching families and coming to the U.S. was part of His plan. The relationships I've built and the community I've found are all part of that. It's clear to me that God is behind all of it.

ONA CURTO

I started going to Church Project in 2017 after moving away from my hometown and leaving everything I knew. I entered into a dark phase in my life filled with hate, lust, and thoughts of self harm. I was stuck in the pit for two years and saw no escape. After denying Christ and later attempting to take my own life, I heard from God. It was clear I needed to run back to my Father. I started to become consistent at Church project. I was no longer just an attendee, but an active participant in Gods Church. I went on my first mission trip after that with no expectations, and God used that to turn my life around. The group of guys that I surrounded myself with loved me so beautifully through all of this, and were there to lead me in the ways I should go, and help me when I struggled. I began to serve twice a month and give consistently. I do this out of the love I have for Church project and more importantly God's church. Jesus used this church to bring me back to him and I'm forever grateful. I want to be able to do for others as Christ used people at Church project to do for me. I'm able to serve here and be fed weekly within House Church. This Church has help me understand what the church is supposed to be. It's the people, it's the community, it's the love we show one another. The beautiful body of believers at Church project is unlike anything I've ever seen or experienced and I'm truly grateful to call in my home Church. I love that.

JEFFREY BLANKENSHIP, FORMER STUDENT
& STUDENT GROUP LEADER

I've been part of Church Project since 2018. I joined as a quiet 7th grader, invited by my cousins to the Monday night youth group. From day one, I felt welcomed and immediately found belonging. As I grew in Project Students, I walked alongside incredible young women, supported each other through struggles, and celebrated our growth in Christ. The girls in my group became my closest friends and accountability partners.

Shannon and Gillian, my leaders, were key in my spiritual growth. Shannon helped me through a season of doubt, listening, praying, and pointing me to Scripture. She helped me see God as someone I could approach with my questions. Gillian challenged me to lead and disciple others, pushing me out of my comfort zone and growing my faith.

Discipling others was one of the most impactful experiences of my time in Project Students. I went through the discipleship process three times, learning that discipleship is about building intentional relationships that point others to Christ. I also led small group discussions with junior high girls, which tested my faith and gave me the chance to pass on the love and encouragement I'd received.

The mission trip to Belize was another defining moment, where I served in Vacation Bible School and construction projects. The relationships I formed there, especially with the children, are among my most cherished memories. The unity of our team, working together for God's Kingdom, was a powerful reminder of the importance of serving.

Being a consistent part of this ministry for 6 years gave me a unique experience within Project Students. The teachings on Monday nights, rooted in Scripture, gave me a hunger for God's Word that has only deepened over time. It is here that I learned to love God's Word. I began to see the Bible not just as a book of rules, but as a living, breathing guide that speaks to every area of my life. The youth group went beyond just teaching us The Word — it helped push us to become more like Jesus and live out what we learned in our day-to-day lives, guiding us in our application of The Word. It is where I found belonging, purpose, and a sense of identity in Christ. It was through this ministry that I was able to overcome doubts, grow in my faith, and become the person God created me to be.

Even now, as a freshman in college, my appreciation for the impact of Project Students has only deepened as I get to return to lead at events like Encounter and Retreat and continue to foster and grow relationships I had formed in my time as a student. I look back on my time in Project Students with gratitude for all the lessons I learned, the relationships I built, and the way God moved in my life. Project Students has not only helped me grow in my faith, but it has also shaped me into the person I am today — a woman who loves God's Word, loves others, and deeply loves the church.

KENDALL MCBRIDE

I've struggled with insecurity and anxiety my whole life. Going to youth group was a huge hurdle, and I'd often decide to stay home instead. One day, I told my mom I thought I was depressed. I didn't know what I was dealing with because no one talked about anything deeper than middle school stuff. I felt like a glitch, completely abnormal, and like my presence wasn't needed.

This darkness led me to a psychiatric facility, where I realized I had to press into Jesus. In a coffee shop, I prayed and gave my life to Jesus. I wish I could say everything got better, but I soon faced spiritual attacks. My mom told me: *Resist the devil and he will flee from you.* That night, I lay in bed feeling overwhelmed, and I heard a voice say *Say my name.* I spoke *Yahweh* and instantly, everything lifted.

Jesus is the *I AM* to me. I wouldn't be where I am without people like Mackenzie, Taylor, and Angela pouring into my life. There's no one to thank for that, but Jesus.

MALLORY RUFF

Jacque: I was focused on my career and worldly goals. We had a loving family but didn't go to church. After Jack was born, he died three times in the hospital and was later diagnosed with cerebral palsy. At family dinners, he would point to the sky and say, "Jesus." Chip and I were confused because we didn't speak Jesus' name at home.

I was lost, wanting to believe in something but unsure what. At three years old, Jack, who was still learning to talk, told me that God sent him to find me because I was lost. Those words came straight from God, and it changed our lives forever. Our family is now all believers, and it's transformed generations to come.

Jack: Everyone faces struggles, but I wish people didn't feel lost all the time. God knew you before He formed you in the womb. He chose you and died for you. He could've destroyed the world and started over, but He didn't.

THE ABERNATHY FAMILY

I grew up in the church and accepted Jesus young, but it wasn't until this year that I truly understood how much I need a savior and how to follow Jesus with everything. At the start of last school year, my Bible teacher asked, "What would it look like if we centered everything around Jesus?" I thought, "That sounds pretty lame." For years, I did what I wanted, putting my worth in others and how I felt. But through what Christ has done for me, I now see how amazing He truly is.

Even when I turned away, Jesus never stopped pursuing me. When the enemy ruled parts of my life, Jesus still wanted me. When I felt ashamed,

He called me worthy. Christ saved me from guilt, shame, confusion, hate, depression, addiction, and death. With Him alive in me, I now walk in freedom, peace, love, joy, and abundance.

I have faith in Jesus because only He can fill my heart. He's called me to love others as He has loved me. I want to be baptized to show that the old is dead and to declare freedom and redemption in Christ. I want my life centered around Jesus, to make my faith my own, and to show others His love and purpose.

KYAH GONZALEZ

In my 5.5 years at Church Project, I've had the privilege of working with 5th-12th graders. I've seen this generation of students hungry for Jesus, eager to follow Him and walk with Him daily. They lead in many ways, disciple each other intentionally, and live the abundant life Jesus speaks of in John 10:10. I believe this generation will change how people see Christ, Christians, and the Church, returning to a biblical model of discipleship, seeking to be disciples rather than just church-goers.

I'm excited for them and honored to serve as their Student Pastor. Again and again, they challenge me in my own spiritual growth and bring me joy as I watch them *belong, believe, become.* I love them and am so grateful for how well they've loved me over these last 5.5 years. Church, your younger brothers and sisters in Christ are ready to carry the mantle — compelled by the Gospel and falling deeply in love with Jesus. I can't wait for you to see them blow you away with the faith and awe they live their lives with.

TREVOR ANDERSON, PROJECT STUDENTS PASTOR

Project Kids: CHURCHPROJECT.ORG/KIDS
Fifty6 Students: CHURCHPROJECT.ORG/FIFTY6
Project Students: CHURCHPROJECT.ORG/STUDENTS

What could we become?

We just celebrated our 15th Staff and Spouse Christmas Party. Every year, our staff, along with their spouses, get together for a really great event. This is one of the few times in the year when we really go next level to show our team how much we appreciate them. It's unashamedly nice, and they deserve it.

During that party, we have a moment where people say some things that they have felt are significant from this past year, or for the year ahead. As is the case every year, and again this year, many on our staff said some profound and encouraging things, things that I often remember, and that mean a lot to everyone in the room.

A couple of things that a couple of our elders said this year really resonated with how I feel. One of our elders noted that 15 years is really just an awkward adolescent age. And that as a church, we're really just still an adolescent. We've grown a lot. But, we're only 15 years old. Another one of our elders said that he believed that 15 years was just the beginning for us. So much has happened, but so much is ahead for us. We have a strong foundation to build on.

This reminded me of something that was said to me earlier this year – prayed over Brooke and me. We hosted an event this year where the speaker was a spiritual leader, who is known and respected globally, whose ministry has quietly impacted millions who have come to faith in Jesus. I have respected this leader from afar for many years. The work this person has been used by God to do has had ripple effects around the world. At this event, the leader and his wife spent some time with Brooke and me. They prayed over us and for us and for the work of Church Project. At the end of prayer, he looked at me and said: *You haven't seen anything yet.* He said that he sensed, from all that he has seen and known in ministry, and from what he understands about Church Project – that this is the start of something that will have impact for the kingdom for a long time, in a lot of places.

This is how I feel. All of these things summarize what I sense. I actually do feel like we're just beginning. I actually do feel like we're just coming of age. I actually do feel like we haven't seen anything yet. I actually do feel like God has so much more in store for us.

For this coming season, my guiding question to our team has been: *What could this become?* Specifically, I have challenged them to pray through and dream about what the ministries that they have been trusted to lead could become. Is what they are leading now all that was meant to be? Is there something more? Could we be healthier? Could we be more effective? Are there more people to reach and affect? What is God saying to us, where is He leading us, and what does He want from us?

And I ask this question for our entire church. My question for Church Project is: *what could this become?* What does God have for us? What is He leading us to do? How can we become healthier? More effective? How can each of us bring more people in to what He is doing here? How are we called to affect more people with what He has entrusted to us?

Surely there are more neighborhoods that need House Churches.

Surely there are ministries that could use more of our support through partnership and finances.

Surely there are more cities that need a church that teaches the Scriptures unashamedly, shares the gospel boldly, lives simply, gives generously, and gathers in committed, diverse, discipleship communities.

Surely there are more neighbors in our communities that need to be brought into a relationship with Christ.

Surely there are more churches around the nation and world that we can encourage and help resource.

As Church Project is turning 15 years old, I am 51. My original dream for my life did not include what I'm doing now. But somehow, I started working at a church the week after I graduated high school, and I haven't stopped. All throughout college, when I was preparing to do other things, I kept working in churches. And here I am now, at 51 years old, having spent most of my life serving in and through the local church.

I've grown so much. God has used this church to mature and refine me. He still has so much more work to do in me. But He uses this church in part to do that. I like to say that I needed so much sanctification, God made me a husband, a father, and a pastor. Church Project continues to be a tool that God uses to sanctify me – making me more like Christ as I die to myself.

When people ask me about what I see ahead for us as Church Project, I usually answer: *more of the same.*

More House Churches planted locally and multiple House Churches in every neighborhood.

More salvations and baptisms because more people are becoming evangelists and having Good.God.Gospel. conversations.

More giving that can be stewarded for the gospel and good works, because more people are surrendering to a life of radical, gospel generosity.

More ministries partnered with to meet needs and share the gospel all throughout our community.

More Church Projects planted around our city, nation, and world.

More resources shared to the global church through tools like Start With 7, Good.God.Gospel., and beyond.

I believe in the beauty and the power of the local church more than ever. I am more committed to my personal calling and to the calling of Church Project, more than I ever have been.

I believe God has entrusted something beautiful to us here. I believe that He started something really special here. And I think that we are privileged to be a part of it. And I think that one day we will look back and see what a privilege it was to join Jesus in His work through this local church.

My calling to each one of us: let's go. Let's not sit still. Let's not regress. Let's go. Let's move forward. Let's love Jesus more than we ever have. Let's love His church more than we ever have. Let's be more surrendered to Him with all of our lives. Let's be more committed to the work of the gospel than ever.

We have one short life. This is a great way to spend it.

Great things have happened. Even greater days are ahead.

You are loved.

JASON SHEPPERD, LEAD PASTOR

Church Project Website:
CHURCHPROJECT.ORG

Church Project Network:
CHURCHPROJECTNETWORK.COM

Give to Church Project:
CHURCHPROJECT.ORG/GIVE

CP APP
(Apple + Google)

GOOD.GOD.GOSPEL.
(Evangelism)

START WITH 7
(Audio Devotionals)

Facebook:
/CHURCHPROJECT

Instagram:
@CHURCHPROJECT

Watch Existing Stories:
YOUTUBE.COM/CHURCHPROJECT

Share Your Story:
CHURCHPROJECT.ORG/STORIES

CHURCH PROJECT
Biblical. Simple. Relevant.

CHURCH
BIBLICAL.SIMPLE.RELEVANT.
PROJECT

Made in the USA
Columbia, SC
08 February 2025

52726544R10121